"This book explores the creative dimensi̤o̤n̤s̤ ̤o̤f̤ ̤G̤o̤d̤'̤s̤ ̤p̤ṳr̤p̤o̤s̤e̤ ̤a̤n̤d̤ ̤m̤e̤a̤n̤i̤n̤g̤ for business. It is a must-read for those who are seeking to glorify God as they do business."

**C. William Pollard,** Chairman Emeritus, The ServiceMaster Company

"In *Why Business Matters to God,* Van Duzer, a lawyer turned business-school dean, treads where most clergy and theologians fear to go, yet where most parishioners must go every day: into the marketplace. Van Duzer resists easy stereotyping and business bashing, opting instead for a careful theological treatment of the role of business in God's created order. Noting the practical good and harm that flow from business in a fallen world, Van Duzer offers theological framing and practical ideas for how business can be redeemed, discover a new purpose and even become a new creation. Van Duzer is to be applauded and his model should be carefully considered by those who choose to be in the world but not of it."

**David W. Miller,** Ph.D., Director, Princeton University Faith & Work Initiative, Associate Research Scholar, and President, The Avodah Institute

"Dean Van Duzer has written an important book and written it well. Born in his own skepticism and refined through years of insightful reflection, his scriptural framework has contributed meaningfully to my understanding and inspires my daily work in the noble calling of business. He achieves his intention of being both affirming and provocative, and the questions he asks will help transform the minds of many as we strive to live into the answers, here, 'between the finish lines.'"

**Barry Rowan,** Executive Vice President, Chief Financial Officer and Chief Administrative Officer, Vonage

"A significant book. Van Duzer lays a solid theological framework for understanding business in the context of God's creativity, human depravity and redemption. Well written and chock-full of vivid vignettes from the marketplace."

**Alec Hill,** President, InterVarsity Christian Fellowship USA, and author of *Just Business: Christian Ethics for the Marketplace*

"Van Duzer skillfully situates the purposes of business in the context of the grand narrative of God's creation, humankind's Fall, and our and the world's ultimate redemption. With a writing style that is both accessible and inviting, he integrates sound theology and 'real world' common sense in addressing the Christian businessperson's endemic search for meaning and motivation in business. Well done!"

**Dr. Mitchell J. Neubert,** Chavanne Chair of Christian Ethics in Business, Baylor University

"I have been looking for a book like this for over twenty years. Now it finally exists. The majority of Christians in the world are engaged in some kind of business activity. Though churches and dozens of books provide helpful guidance on how to do business in ethical ways, tragically, very few offer insight into why God would have someone do business at all. This book lays a solid and practical foundation for a theological understanding of God's purposes for business and in so doing issues a prophetic challenge: maximizing profit isn't even on the list of God's purposes for business. Rather, God has far deeper and more life-giving reasons to call people to business. Drawing on the author's rich experience both in the 'business' of law and as the dean of a remarkable Christian business school, on his theological studies, and on his exceptional skill as an educator and communicator, this book is a feast of spiritual insights, business case studies and very practical implications. It deserves to be a must-read for Christians in business, for business courses in colleges and business schools, and for church fellowship groups."

**Tim Dearborn,** Director of Christian Commitments, World Vision International

*"Why Business Matters to God* is thought-provoking. It is a theological review of 'the beginning,' 'the Fall' and 'the restoration' of God's image bearers and the resulting struggle for those engaged in business who desire to honor God. Van Duzer logically and persuasively makes the case that such business necessities as being efficient and profitable should be subordinate to the foremost responsibility of serving the public— an achievable calling, with prayer and the Holy Spirit's help."

**Richard C. Chewning,** Emeritus Professor of Christian Ethics, Baylor University

"It would be hard to imagine a better book on business from a Christian perspective. *Why Business Matters to God* is solidly biblical, deeply theological and realistically practical. It is a must-read not only for all Christians in business but also for pastors and other church leaders who are committed to helping the people of God live each day for God's purposes in the world."

**Mark D. Roberts,** Senior Director and Scholar-in-Residence, Laity Lodge, Texas

"Jeff Van Duzer has written an incredibly important book on a subject that, in recent years, has generated much more heat than light. Finally, we have a substantive, relevant book that articulates a theology of business that is both rich and practical. With clear insights derived from Scripture and the world of business, Van Duzer advances a vision for companies and their leaders that is purposeful, profitable and sustainable. He calls all of us to action by showing that we need a different way of doing business. *Why Business Matters to God* shows us how we can move forward, and it should be required reading for anyone in business who cares about the common good."

**D. Michael Lindsay,** author of *Faith in the Halls of Power*

"No business school faculty has done a better job of exploring the integration of Christian faith and values with the education of business managers than Seattle Pacific University under the leadership of Dean Jeff Van Duzer. *Why Business Matters to God* walks its readers through key biblical texts and themes on the one hand, and today's business challenges and opportunities on the other. Van Duzer interacts creatively with some of the best classic and contemporary thinkers on the subject of faith and work. A good and important read for business veterans as well as students and recent grads."

**David W. Gill,** Mockler-Phillips Professor of Workplace Theology & Business Ethics, Gordon-Conwell Theological Seminary, and author of *It's About Excellence* and *Doing Right*

# Why Business Matters to God

## (And What Still Needs to Be Fixed)

# JEFF VAN DUZER

IVP Academic

An imprint of InterVarsity Press
Downers Grove, Illinois

*InterVarsity Press*
*P.O. Box 1400, Downers Grove, IL 60515-1426*
*World Wide Web: www.ivpress.com*
*E-mail: email@ivpress.com*

*InterVarsity Press® is the book-publishing division of InterVarsity Christian Fellowship/USA®, a movement of students and faculty active on campus at hundreds of universities, colleges and schools of nursing in the United States of America, and a member movement of the International Fellowship of Evangelical Students. For information about local and regional activities, write Public Relations Dept., InterVarsity Christian Fellowship/USA, 6400 Schroeder Rd., P.O. Box 7895, Madison, WI 53707-7895, or visit the IVCF website at <www.intervarsity.org>.*

*Design: Cindy Kiple*
*Images: Robert Daly/Getty Images*

*ISBN 978-0-8308-3888-2*

*Printed in the United States of America* ∞

 *InterVarsity Press is committed to protecting the environment and to the responsible use of natural resources. As a member of Green Press Initiative we use recycled paper whenever possible. To learn more about the Green Press Initiative, visit <www.greenpressinitiative.org>.*

**Library of Congress Cataloging-in-Publication Data**

*Van Duzer, Jeffrey B.*
  *Why business matters to God: (and what still needs to be fixed) /*
*Jeff Van Duzer.*
      *p. cm.*
  *Includes bibliographical references and index.*
  *ISBN 978-0-8308-3888-2 (pbk.: alk. paper)*
  *1. Business—Religious aspects—Christianity. I. Title.*
  *HF5388.V36 2010*
  *261.8'5—dc22*

                                                                    *2010024974*

**P**  20  19  18  17  16  15  14  13  12  11  10  9  8  7  6  5  4  3  2

**Y**  27  26  25  24  23  22  21  20  19  18  17  16  15  14  13  12

*To my wonderful colleagues
in the School of Business and Economics
at Seattle Pacific University*

# Contents

# Preface and Acknowledgments

This book is about why business can be, and often is, a powerful tool for good in the hands of God. It is a book that celebrates the amazing way that the market works, and it sees global capitalism as one of the best hopes for addressing the problems of the world. It is a book that seeks to honor Christians who have been called into business and who have often been made to feel like second-class citizens in God's kingdom. It seeks to affirm the intrinsic value of business work as work full of meaning and importance to God.

However, it is also a book that argues that, for all the good that business is already doing in the world, it could do more. It seeks to challenge the dominant business paradigm of the day. It argues that a true understanding of Scripture requires that a number of assumptions that are often taken as givens be reexamined and, in many cases, turned upside down.

As such, this book seeks to encourage and challenge at the same time. It is intended to provide business persons with a framework that will allow them to see the importance of their daily work from God's perspective and at the same time, call them to more carefully align their practices with God's grand plans for humanity. In short the book is trying to be both comforting and prophetic, to describe both why business matters to God and why there is still more work to be done.

I am extremely grateful for the friends and counselors who have guided me along this path. In particular, I wish to thank my colleagues in the School of Business and Economics at Seattle Pacific University who have worked with me for many years to help develop the thoughts that I have set forth in this book. In truth, it might be fairer to list us collectively as the authors of this book—except that that would end up saddling them with the errors that I have, no doubt, made, and that would suggest a somewhat greater uniformity of views on all particulars than would be fair. I would also like to express my gratitude to my colleagues in Seattle Pacific's School of Theology who have worked closely with our School of Business for years in commenting on, refining and shaping our thinking—thinking which has now found its way into this book.

I am also very grateful to many friends in business, the church and the academy who have offered me counsel, read manuscripts and pushed my thinking along the way. In particular, I want to thank Dan Baumgartner, Barry Rowan and Doug Strong for their willingness to read multiple drafts and to suggest meaningful correction and improvements. I am also grateful for the assistance and encouragement of Mike Purdy, Tim Dearborn, Gary Karns, Cindy Strong and Bruce Hansen (and the men in his Bible study group).

Finally, I must thank my family for their patience in hearing me out as I talked about these ideas ad nauseam. I thank them for their support through some of the slower parts of the process and for their constant encouragement. In particular, this book would not have happened without the loving care of my wife, Margie, to whom I am for this, and so much more, eternally grateful.

# Introduction

In many ways I am an unlikely author of a book on why business matters to God.

I grew up just outside of Berkeley, California, and went to high school there during the late 1960s and early 1970s. These were radical times in a radicalized place, and I was steeped in the "anti" ethos of the day. It was in the air we breathed—a kind of backdrop for all the usual traumas of adolescence. We were against the war in Vietnam. We were against the police. We were against the government. Indeed, we were against authority of any kind. Authority was "the man" and one could either actively resist it or just "turn on, tune in and drop out."

In this cultural milieu we were, of course, also against capitalism and business. Even without knowing where I learned this, I came to believe almost unconsciously (and certainly uncritically) that business and market economies were the source of much damage and evil in the world. Greedy capitalists were polluting the environment. Big business was profiting from the war and encouraging its continuation. Discrimination against blacks and women was rampant. Large international businesses were plundering the poor in what we referred to in those days as "third-world countries." And so on. Moreover as a Christian I was sure that God would agree with these assessments. A radical Jesus would want the tables of these money changers and merchants overthrown and the business leaders driven from the temple.

If you had told me as I graduated from high school that someday I would be the dean of a business school, I would have told you that you must be smoking something. (And in those days you probably would have been.)

Fast forward thirty years. After a number of different moves in my life, that in retrospect primarily prove that God is sovereign and has a tremendous sense of humor, in 2001 I was appointed the fourth dean of Seattle Pacific University's business school. SPU is a Christian university affiliated with the Free Methodist denomination. All of its faculty subscribe to a broadly ecumenical Christian faith statement, and I soon discovered that they took their faith very seriously. For the first time in my life I found myself working in a setting that invited me to think deeply and clearly about the discipline of business from God's perspective.

## HOW IT GOT STARTED

Against this backdrop, a few early discoveries served as the seeds for many of the thoughts that I want to share in this book. First, I realized that from my adolescence I still had a well-rehearsed litany of critiques that I could lay at the doorstep of business. But now I was the dean of a business school. I was regularly being invited to speak on business to student groups, cross-campus gatherings, Rotary clubs and other community groups from the perspective of a champion and apologist. These folks wanted to know what was going on in our school and how the business leaders we were training would be agents for affirmative, life-giving change in the world. It became apparent to me that I had some work to do.

I set out to learn what I could say that was positive about business—and somewhat to my surprise, I discovered that I didn't have to look far. What I quickly learned was that my high school prejudices were in some cases simply wrong and in almost every case woefully one-sided. I began to meet with Christian business leaders who told me stories of how they went to extraordinary lengths to care for employees who were going through difficult patches in their lives. They talked about how their businesses gave them opportunities to serve in different ways in their communities. They showed me how the products they were making were bringing health to sick people and Internet access to those who for centuries had not been able to get the information they needed. Most of all they shared with me the sense of joy and fulfillment that they were finding in their day-to-day work.

I also began to read about examples of business behavior around the globe and realized how business generates the economic capital that allows the rest of society to flourish. I saw small-scale examples of how modest loans and investments proved sufficient to launch economically prosperous communities. I saw how businesses often provided opportunities that never before existed so that, for example, young girls could now receive an education that was previously out of reach. I observed the benefits to larger economies when new businesses entered the market and allowed the community to become less dependent on a single industry. I found case after case where businessmen and women were playing leadership roles in pursuing systems and structures designed to better protect human rights. I discovered that many companies were on the forefront of efforts to address global climate change. In short, I found much to celebrate about the role of business in the world.

Of course, not everything was rosy. This was all unfolding for me at the same time that we were navigating through the collapse of Enron and the massive malfeasance of WorldCom, Tyco and many others. But to me, the good that business was doing did not get washed away in the wake of these failures. Instead, it stood out all the more—at least pointing the way toward a positive understanding of the role of business in society. I found myself often replacing my earlier reflexive criticisms of business with a more balanced view. Indeed, at times I found myself in danger of exhibiting a zealotry in defense of business that often characterizes the fervor of the recent convert.

A second early discovery was far less happy, however. When I met with business leaders I would sometimes ask them how their identities as Christians changed how they did their work. In other words, what difference did it make to their work that they were Christians? Unfortunately, far too frequently, the answer that I got back was some variant of "Well, Jeff, business is business, but I try to be honest and kind." In other words, everyone does business the same way.[1] There is nothing any more particular about Christian business than there would be about the molecular formula ($H_2O$) that a Christian scientist would use to make water from hydrogen and oxygen. Being a Christian means doing the same work everyone else was doing but just trying to be nicer about it—a perspective that I have come to describe disparagingly as "Enron with a smile." And I found myself asking if this really was all that Christianity has to say about the practice of business.

My conversations with these business leaders also revealed another factor that has animated this book. Quite often, these leaders felt ignored or treated like second-class citizens in their churches and in the broader Christian community. They told me that they would never ask for business advice from their pastors since their pastors would have nothing to tell them about how to make Christian business decisions. Their pastors didn't understand business and didn't seem particularly interested in learning. Indeed, at times business was characterized from the pulpit as the expression of sinful greed—perhaps a necessary evil but certainly nothing to be encouraged. A calling to business was always put in third place behind a calling to a position in the church or the mission field or a calling to one of the "helping professions"—a designation that incidentally never included business. Their work was never celebrated in the church community. When they got a promotion nobody at their church ever suggested a commissioning service for them. Conversely, many heard sermon examples of "exemplary Christians" who left successful business practices to go to the mission field. The message was clear. One serves God by leaving business. Apparently what was once sordid or at best neutral could now be redeemed in so-called full-time Christian service.[2]

---

[1]As one longtime business consultant and counselor scoffed, "There is no such thing as a Christian business. *Christian* is better used as a noun than an adjective" (quoted in Laura Nash, *Believers in Business* [Nashville: Thomas Nelson, 1994], p. 24).

[2]This sense of disenfranchisement has been well documented in the literature. See, for example, R. Paul Stevens, *Doing God's Business: Meaning and Motivation for the Marketplace* (Grand Rapids: Eerdmans, 2006), p.79; D. Michael Lindsay, *Faith in the Halls of Power: How Evangelicals*

In short, many owners and managers of businesses seem to feel disenfranchised from God's work in the world. For most of their working hours these businessmen and women feel only indirectly connected to what God is doing. For them, business is at best an instrumental means to an end. They work for most of their lives at what they characterize as essentially neutral activities. With the money they earn, however, they can support a missionary, a local church or a not-for-profit ministry—that is they can fund the "real work" of God in the world. Their part in God's grand scheme is limited to providing resources to others and, along the way, abiding by a personal code of ethics that calls them to act with integrity and kindness. In effect, God's sacred realm invades their secular activities only at the level of personal behavior. Work (and its products) remain neatly divided between the secular (which hardly counts) and the sacred (which is ultimately all that matters). But this is a false dichotomy and bad theology that limits the advance of God's kingdom.

These discoveries led me and my colleagues to begin a multiyear effort to find and read what had been written on these subjects. Specifically, we began to ask how God sees business. If God has a role for it at all, what would God want business to be about? What should it do—that is, what is its purpose? And what should it not do—what are its limits?

Remarkably from our standpoint, when we began this effort we found very little written that discussed these issues at a macro level (although much more has been written recently). We found a modest amount written about a theology of work and more written on a biblical understanding of money and wealth accumulation.[3] We found a number of useful resources about personal ethics in the workplace but little

---

*Joined the American Elite* (New York: Oxford University Press, 2007), pp. 161-65, 195; David Miller, *God at Work: The History and Promise of the Faith at Work Movement* (New York: Oxford University Press, 2007), pp. 9-13, 63, 91-93.

[3]On a theology of work see, for example, D. Sherman and W. Hendricks, *Your Work Matters to God* (Colorado Springs: NavPress, 1987), and Lee Hardy, *The Fabric of This World* (Grand Rapids: Eerdmans, 1990). On money and wealth accumulation see Ron Sider, *Rich Christians in an Age of Hunger* (Downers Grove, Ill.: InterVarsity Press, 1977); and Randy Alcorn, *Money, Possessions and Eternity* (Wheaton, Ill.: Tyndale House, 1989).

or no work on building the underlying theological framework for the discipline as a whole.[4]

The purpose of this book is to encourage conversation around the development of such a theological framework. I am not writing to criticize the church (or for that matter, Christians in business). Other recent works have begun to explore why those trained in theology and pastoral ministry often have difficulties providing helpful advice to their parishioners on business issues.[5] Nor would I want to claim that this book represents the first efforts to explore a theology of business. I am clearly "writing on the shoulders" of a number who have gone before and who have written about business issues and on related theologies of work and wealth.[6] Still, at least relative to other theological inquiries and to the development of systems of ethics, the theological foundation for an understanding of business remains underdeveloped.[7]

## SEVERAL TENSIONS

As this project has unfolded three sets of tensions have arisen. The first should have been obvious to me from the beginning. This book is interdisciplinary; in it I hope to connect theological and biblical studies, on

---

[4]On personal ethics see, for example, Alexander Hill, *Just Business: Christian Ethics for the Marketplace* (Downers Grove, Ill.: InterVarsity Press, 1997); Richard C. Chewning, John W. Eby and Shirley J. Roels, *Business Through the Eyes of Faith* (San Francisco: Harper & Row, 1990).

[5]See generally Miller, *God at Work;* Laura Nash and Scotty McLennan, *Church on Sunday, Work on Monday: The Challenge of Fusing Christian Values with Business Life* (San Francisco: Jossey-Bass, 2001).

[6]Several authors have written sociological works analyzing how Christians in business actually behave. These include Nash, *Believers in Business;* Miller, *God at Work;* and Lindsay, *Faith in the Halls of Power.* Others have approached the subject more theoretically, developing and laying out theological insights. See, for example, Stevens, *Doing God's Business;* Michael Novak, *Business as a Calling: Work and the Examined Life* (New York: Free Press, 1996); Richard C. Chewning, ed., *Biblical Principles and Business: The Foundations* (Colorado Springs: NavPress, 1989); Helen Alford and Michael Naughton, *Managing as If Faith Mattered: Christian Social Principles in the Modern Organization* (Notre Dame, Ind.: University of Notre Dame Press, 2001). The Alford and Naughton work is a particularly rigorous and well-developed work drawing on Catholic social principles to establish, in effect, a theology of management.

[7]"Amazingly little theological reflection has taken place in the past about an activity which takes up so much of our time. The number of pages theologians have devoted to transubstantiation—which does or does not take place on Sunday—for instance, would, I suspect far exceed the number of pages devoted to work that fills our lives Monday through Saturday" (Miroslav Volf, *Work in the Spirit: Toward a Theology of Work* [Eugene, Ore.: Wipf & Stock, 2001], p. 69).

the one hand, with the disciplines of business and economics, on the other. From my experience, however, interdisciplinary work is often disappointing to practitioners and scholars because it inevitably lacks the depth that could be brought to bear in a work that focuses on a single discipline. Scholars in both disciplines will no doubt wish for more explanations and nuance in some of what follows.

More importantly, however, interdisciplinary work not only seeks to combine the expertise from different fields, it necessarily tries to bring different ethoses—different scholarly cultures—together. Different fields have grown up essentially alone. As such, over time they have developed their own ways of looking at the world, of asking questions, of using language, of pursuing truth. Embedded in these disciplinary silos are essentially different worldviews. Any interdisciplinary work, however, will require that these cultures leave their silos and coexist in the same room. Anyone who has ever met the parents of his or her child's future spouse for the first time may have some sense of the awkwardness of this endeavor. Each family brings years of their own traditions, memories and histories to the meeting, but now in anticipation of the upcoming nuptials these family cultures will, at least periodically, need to learn to coexist and blend together.

I had the great privilege of having several of my colleagues in business and theology read an early draft of this text. Their responses were very helpful but also illustrative of these different worldviews. My business associates criticized the text as being too negative about business. As one suggested, at times this reads like "a left-leaning author who was grudgingly dragged into business and was fighting it, trying to justify his presence there, or, at a minimum, change the ugly capitalistic world in which he found himself." My theology friends, however, argued just the opposite. I was insufficiently sensitive to the legitimate critiques that have been directed at business down through the centuries and unduly positive about businesses' current work in the world. Nowhere did these views clash more directly than in the discussion of profit-making and a market economy— which is why I have sought to devote additional space to these particular features of business in today's global economy in what follows.

The second tension reflects some of the structural challenges inherent in reflecting theologically on what is essentially an applied discipline. I did not set out to write a bifurcated book—a book where the first half was all about the Bible and theology, and the second half was all about business. I wanted to integrate the two from the outset.

The structural challenge, however, arose from my decision to approach this topic by looking separately at each of the movements—the "chapters"—of the big story of Scripture. As I will explain at greater length, I have found it useful to approach the biblical story by looking separately at creation, Fall, redemption and consummation. I believe that together these four movements make up the big story but that each of them contributes new insights into how God sees business today. Consequently, there is value in reflecting on each of them one by one.

In a very real sense, however, I also believe that we will need to consider the whole story in order to fully appreciate its implications for the purpose and practice of business. A consideration of creation independent of the Fall will end up ignoring much of the reality of today's world. Considering the Fall without considering Christ's crucifixion and resurrection will leave us unduly hopeless. Similarly, considering Christ's work at the cross without reflecting on God's "end game" will provide us with only a partial picture of how we are called to live in light of the new creation. In each case, while there are helpful observations to be gleaned from the individual movements, the fullest understanding of Scripture's teaching can only be appreciated from the vantage point of the story in its entirety. In other words, we can best answer some of the big questions about business only after the whole story has been told.

So, I have compromised. In each of the first four chapters I consider one of the four movements of the story. And in each case I end the chapter by briefly highlighting some implications for business and for Christians in the for-profit world. Hopefully this will allow me to highlight some of the implications that flow from that piece of the story and will prove at least minimally sufficient for those readers who are eager to get on to the application.

Only in the last two chapters, however—after the whole story has been told—do I set out in a more comprehensive fashion how all of this applies to business. In chapter seven, the penultimate chapter, I identify an overall framework for business that builds on my earlier discussion of the biblical narrative. Then, in chapter eight, I set forth answers to key philosophical and practical questions that may arise as Christians seek to live out this approach in their places of work.

So, it is my hope that you will find helpful insights in what follows on a chapter-by-chapter basis. But I also hope that you will be rewarded with a richer and fuller understanding by persevering to the end.

The third tension emerged from the dual purpose of this book. In short, I hope that this book can play both a priestly and prophetic role. But there seems to be an inherent tension between these two functions.

In the Old Testament, one of the functions of the priest was to pronounce God's blessing. I hope this book will help business practitioners better understand that their daily work is blessed by God, has great significance for God's work in the world and is consequently endued with great meaning. By providing a conceptual framework for understanding business from God's perspective, I hope to help Christians in business better understand the *sacred* nature of their daily tasks. In short, I hope this book serves as a useful reminder that a calling into business is a noble, kingdom-advancing calling.

To this end, this book seeks to affirm that the day-to-day, seemingly mundane tasks often associated with running a business can indeed be tools that God uses to achieve kingdom objectives. Of course, these tasks often look similar when performed by Christians and non-Christians. Analyzing a spreadsheet, preparing a quarterly income statement and entering into a lease agreement are acts that from the standpoint of the outside observer may look the same regardless of the faith of the practitioner. But from the inside it makes all the difference. If Christians can understand that the work they are doing is God's work they can bring a sense of joy, meaning, purpose, pride and hope to their tasks that might otherwise elude them. In a world where there is a "meaning crisis" in so many work places, hopefully this theological framework can be a valuable help.

In its priestly role, then, this book seeks to pronounce God's blessing on the work *as it is currently being done*. It seeks to affirm that God *is using* business for divine purposes—in effect, that God likes business and values the work of women and men in business.

But the book also hopes to play a prophetic role. Yes, God likes business but God also has purposes and plans for business that we can align with or oppose. While wanting desperately to affirm the kingdom nature of business work, I also do not want to be guilty of just sprinkling holy water on all business practices.

Specifically, by providing an alternative paradigm to the existing emphasis on maximizing profits at all costs, I hope that I can actually play a small part in redirecting the flow and impact of business activities. Business need not be just business as usual. There are alternatives. It can be conceived of and practiced differently, and these differences matter. By focusing on a consideration of business from God's perspective, I am also hoping to engender deeper thinking about the purpose and practice of business that will, where appropriate, lead to *on-the-ground changes in behavior*.

So throughout what follows you may experience the tension that I have encountered as I have sought to pursue these two goals. On the one hand I hope that what I have written can be a life-giving affirmation to a whole class of Christians who for too long have felt like their work had, at best, only instrumental value to God. To this end I simply want to affirm what is. On the other hand I do believe that the dominant paradigm that governs much of our business practices today is flawed and needs to be changed. I seek to call Christians to be at the forefront of these changes. Affirming and challenging. Priest and prophet.

## WHY IT MATTERS

The twenty-first century is destined to be the century of global business. More than any other institution, business is likely to shape the face of our world. The sheer magnitude of the resources controlled by corporations makes it almost certain that business will dwarf the influence of other traditional institutions. Of the 150 largest economies in the world, nearly half are not countries. They are businesses.[8] Annual sales from the top two hundred corporations are larger than the combined economies of all but the twenty-five largest countries in the world.[9] Moreover, businesses are increasingly multinational or transnational in reach. Notwithstanding the retraction in global trade and investment accompanying the 2008-2009 recession, it is very unlikely that we will see a long-term diminution of the cross-border influence of companies. In short, companies doing business will, in many ways, dictate the kind of world we will live in. Thus, for Christians interested in advancing God's agenda of peace, justice and reconciliation, a focus on business and its role in society is critical.

---

[8]Fortune 500 list of companies for 2008 (2007 revenues) <www.money.cnn.com/magazines/fortune/fortune500/2008/full_list/index.html> compared to the "World Economic Outlook Report, October 2008" of the International Monetary Fund for "GDP, current prices" by country for 2007 <www.imf.org/external/pubs/ft/weo/2008/02/weodata/index.aspx>.
[9]Ibid.

# 1

# In the Beginning

Consider an unfinished parable: Three students make appointments to ask a pastor for career advice. The first student explains that she is considering going to law school and asks the pastor why God might want a Christian to be a lawyer. After thinking about her question for a moment, the pastor answers that Christians in law make sense because God cares about justice. By becoming a lawyer she can help advance God's desire for a just society. The second student explains that he is considering a career in medicine and asks why God might want Christians to serve as doctors or nurses. "That's simple," the pastor replies, "God cares about wholeness, and by pursuing a career in the medical field you can play a key part in God's healing work in the world." The last student arrives for her appointment and says she is considering a career in business. She asks the pastor why God might want her to pursue such a career.

At this point, however, the parable remains unfinished. How should the pastor respond? If law furthers God's interest in justice and medicine furthers God's interest in healing, what aspect of God's work will a business career further? Or, put differently, from God's perspective what is the purpose of business?

## GOD'S PURPOSE FOR BUSINESS

Answering this question is not as simple as it may seem at first. Indeed, on closer examination, this one question raises three other preliminary questions.

First, does it even make sense to talk about God having a purpose for business? Or does God only have a purpose for *people* in business? Stated more generally, does God have purposes for institutions? Or is it better to understand institutions (such as corporations, economic systems, governments) as merely artificial human constructs that are in and of themselves inherently neutral—they can further or thwart God's desires depending on the intentions and actions of the human beings within them, but as separate things they are of no account.

Second, setting aside for the moment the question of institutions, what do we mean when we ask about God's purpose for people in business?[1] The Westminster Shorter Catechism (1674) begins this way:

*Question 1.* What is the chief end of man?

*Answer.* Man's chief end is to glorify God and to enjoy him forever.

Is this all that we can say about God's purpose for people active in business? Does God simply have a general purpose for men and women—to glorify and enjoy God—that they are to faithfully pursue across all of their activities? Or can we say something more? Are there any unique purposes that God would like to see accomplished through business activities?

And finally, assuming that God has unique purposes for people in business, are these purposes intrinsic to the actual business activity or only instrumental? For example, businesses can make money for their owners, who in turn can use that money to support mission activities. In this sense businesses could be said to serve God's purposes *instrumentally.* They generate the funds necessary to sponsor God's desired activity.

Businesses can also serve as a platform from which Christians can share their faith with others. Here too is a use for business. *Instrumentally,* it creates a forum for the sharing of the gospel. But still, this is not intrinsic to business itself. Christians are called on to "be prepared to

---

[1]For convenience and flow of argument, I have elected to treat the question of God's purpose for institutions as a stand-alone discussion in chap. 6.

give an answer to everyone who asks" about their faith regardless of the setting (1 Peter 3:15). In the supermarket, on the sidelines of soccer fields, in PTSA meetings as well as in work settings, Christians are invited to share the good news sensitively with all who might be interested in hearing. This fact, however, does not tell us much about how God intends to use the practice of business itself.

Specifically, can we say that business activities—analyzing balance sheets, manufacturing products, marketing goods, providing performance reviews—in and of themselves further God's kingdom?[2] Does business have an *intrinsic* as well as *instrumental* purpose?

## THE SEARCH FOR PURPOSE

Searching for biblically based answers to these questions is not easy. In a narrow verse-by-verse sense there is not much to work with. One can find a handful of ethical admonitions such as the Old Testament's prescription against using faulty scales to apportion out purchased grain (Proverbs 11:1) or the New Testament's admonitions to pay a worker his or her just due (Luke 10:7). Unfortunately, even in the aggregate these prove to be fairly thin threads from which to weave a whole theology. While there is certainly a great deal of teaching in Scripture on economics and a regular call to fair dealing, there is very little written directly about the purpose of business activities, the appropriate limits of business and its role, if any, in God's work in the world.

Consequently, rather than seeking to construct a theology of business from a handful of specific verses, I have found it more useful to build on what has sometimes been called the "grand narrative." All of

---

[2]I make repeated references throughout this book to the "kingdom of God," "God's kingdom" or words to that effect. By this I mean simply the place or places where God reigns, where God is king. The characteristics of this kingdom are the subject of numerous parables and other biblical teaching. While perhaps not all-encompassing, Paul Stevens identifies four key features of God's kingdom: "First, [the kingdom of God] brings the forgiveness of sins. . . . Second, the kingdom brings healing and recovery of full life: 'the blind receive their sight, the lame walk, the lepers are cleansed, the deaf hear, the dead are raised, and the poor have good news brought to them.' . . . Third, the kingdom restores community by providing an open table for sharing meals with sinners, with poor and rich. . . . Finally, Jesus denounced collective, institutional and structural sin . . . especially for the effect it had on the poor and the oppressed" (R. Paul Stevens, *Doing God's Business* [Grand Rapids: Eerdmans, 2006], pp. 84-85).

Scripture (through many writings and in many genres) tells one basic story—one basic story in four great movements.

In the beginning God created a world and placed human beings at its center (creation). It was God's intent to enjoy creation and live in a loving intimacy with humankind forever. This initial intent, however, was thwarted by human disobedience (the Fall). All the rest of the story is about reconciliation. God seeks to reestablish the love relationship that was intended from the beginning (redemption). These efforts climax with God's arrival in the person of Jesus Christ, who breaks down the wall of separation through his death and resurrection and inaugurates the new creation. The full implications of this victory are revealed in the last chapters of the story, the final conclusion (consummation).

The choice of a narrative hermeneutic and the identification of these four great movements of Scripture is certainly not the only option. Theology can be shaped in a number of crucibles. For example, many theologians work in fields of moral, historical or practical theologies. Even for those committed to a biblical theology, there can be many different organizing principles. And to make matters more complicated, even among those adopting a narrative approach to their biblical theologies, there are differences over how to divide the Scriptures into separate movements.[3]

My choice of narrative is partially tactical, as "story" seems to be one of the most effective means of communicating truth in our current cultural environment. Hopefully it is also an ecumenical approach. While the creation-fall-redemption-consummation framework is often associated with the Reformed tradition, as a basic outline of the biblical story it can be adopted by a wide variety of Christian faith traditions. Indeed down through the history of the church this has been a standard way to describe the Christian journey. The emphasis placed on each movement may differ slightly from tradition to tradition (and the implications that follow from these differing emphases may be nontrivial), but still as a basic outline of the overall

---

[3]See, for example, N. T. Wright, "How Can the Bible Be Authoritative?" *NTWrightpage* <www .ntwrightpage.com/Wright_Bible_Authoritative.htm> (creation, fall, Israel, Jesus, church).

biblical narrative, this approach should allow for different traditions to find common ground.[4]

In the context of this grand narrative, then, it makes sense to begin our search for purpose with a consideration of the creation movement. After all, the creation account describes the world as God originally intended it to be. While the Fall interfered with this plan (and will need to be considered separately), it is still useful to start by considering what God had in mind at the very beginning.

## THE BREVITY OF THE CREATION ACCOUNT

When we think of the Scripture story as comprising four grand movements, it is remarkable that the description of the first two of the four movements is completed by the end of the third chapter of the first book. Creation is described in Genesis 1–2.[5] The Fall is described in Genesis 3. Everything else in Scripture—the remainder of Genesis, the remaining thirty-eight books in the Old Testament and all of the New Testament—is given over to the great third movement of redemption and the fourth movement of consummation.

For our purposes the very brevity of the creation account should serve as an important reminder. First, it reminds us that God is most fully known in redemptive activity. In some ways, virtually the entire Bible tells the story of God's efforts to restore the relationships that God desired from the beginning. It is a story of love—a love that is expressed in a constant reaching out, a grace that seeks communion with a rebellious people, consistently offering them that which they do not deserve. A theology of business must be set, first and foremost, in the context of God's desire to restore this loving relationship.

Second, as we turn to the "creation movement" itself, the sheer brev-

---

[4]My choice of this particular approach is also a reflection of my own heritage. I have grown up as a Protestant primarily in evangelical Presbyterian churches. Consciously or otherwise, I'm sure that I bring a Reformed perspective to this project, hopefully tempered in part by my current happy assignment in a Wesleyan institution.

[5]Additional poetic accounts of God's creation can be found in the Psalms and are alluded to elsewhere in the Scriptures. Still Genesis 1-2 remains the primary account of God's initial work at creation.

ity of this section of Scripture must give us pause as we seek to draw conclusions about God's original plan. Here we find only the slightest of hints, almost imperceptible nods toward various aspects of divine truth. On the one hand, this brevity invites us to speculate from the tiniest of clues. On the other hand, it reminds us that for the most part we are speculating. The terse account reinforces our need for humility, reminding us that we must wrap our conclusions in a cloak of tentativeness. Much of the meaning of the creation story will necessarily remain shrouded in mystery.

## OBSERVATIONS FROM CREATION

With these cautions in mind, then, let us consider what observations we might make from the account of creation.

*1. The material world matters to God.* The observation that the material world matters to God is so obvious that it would be easy to overlook. Throughout the Genesis account of creation God makes material things, and each is declared good. Clearly, the material world matters to God. When God conceives of human flourishing, it involves, in part, the satisfaction of the material needs and desires of men and women.[6] Food that nourishes, roofs that hold out the rain, shade that protects from the heat of the sun—these are all part of God's good design. When businesses produce material things that

---

[6]In this book I make repeated references to "human flourishing," but this is a difficult concept to reduce to a simple definition. At its heart, a human being flourishes when he or she moves toward becoming more the person God designed him or her to be. As such, this notion has a developmental character. It implies growth and change. Human flourishing also taps into the notion of biblical abundance. Jesus assures his followers that he has come "that they might have life, and have it to the full" (John 10:10). But it is a multidimensional abundance. It includes the spiritual, physical, intellectual, aesthetic, emotional and social aspects of our lives. It does not consist of the mere accumulation of more things—particularly when such accumulation comes at the cost of the development of other human dimensions. On the other hand, it is not merely a spiritual concept. It is not just limited, for example, to the cultivation of the gifts of the Spirit. As I have argued in the text, the material world (and the physical goods derived therefrom) matters to God. Our physical well-being is a part of human flourishing. It is also not a solitary concept. It contextualizes individual well-being within a community. A rich understanding of human flourishing acknowledges that individuals are made for relationships. While it recognizes the value and dignity of each individual, it also affirms that individual development must be grounded in community.

enhance the welfare of the community, they are engaged in work that matters to God.

**2. Human beings are called to steward God's creation.** The Genesis account reminds us that the world was made by God and remains God's creation. God made the heavens and the earth. God turned on the lights. God parted the waters to bring forth the sky as well as dry land. God made plants and wildlife, and for a finale, made human beings.

Nowhere in the account is there any suggestion, however, that title to creation was somehow then transferred to Adam and Eve. The only things given to them outright were "seed-bearing plants" and "fruits with seeds," and these were only made available to them as food (Genesis 1:29). By the double reference to "seeds," the account suggests that even in this provision for them, God did not intend to relinquish the ongoing productive capacity of God's creation to human beings. They could eat the fruit, and the plants would continue to grow more fruit. In effect, Adam and Eve were invited to enjoy the income from God's trust without invading the principal. God remained the owner. As the psalmist reminds us:

> The earth is the LORD's, and everything in it,
> > the world, and all who live in it;
> for he founded it upon the seas
> > and established it upon the waters. (Psalm 24:1-2)

This is not to say, however, that Adam and Eve were mere passive beneficiaries of God's largesse. They were given a role to play. In a shorthand way we can identify this role as one of "stewards" or in more modern parlance "trustees." A steward (or trustee) is "a person who manages another's property or financial affairs; one who administers anything as the agent of another."[7] Human beings were called to steward God's creation on God's behalf. "The LORD God took the man and put him in the Garden of Eden to work it and take care of it" (Genesis 2:15).

For Christians in business, acknowledging their role as stewards is

---

[7]*Dictionary.com*, s.v. "stewardship," <www.dictionary.reference.com>.

an important first step toward understanding God's intentions for business. Implicit in this acknowledgment is the conviction that the business does not belong to them or to any other earthly owners. It belongs to God. This sets the frame through which any consideration of shareholder or stakeholder rights must be viewed.

Of course, this is not the end of the inquiry. It is not enough just to conclude that we act as stewards of God's creation. This conclusion invites the next question: if we are to manage creation for God's purposes, what end should we be pursuing? What does the owner want us to do with the "trust corpus"?

Consider, by analogy, a family trust established today. In law, the trustee who agrees to administer the trust for the family is bound to follow the instructions of the one who formed and funded the trust, the trust's "settlor." These instructions are usually set forth in a trust agreement. To the extent that the agreement is silent on certain points, the law will fill in the gaps by implying certain duties for the trustee. For example, by law a trustee owes the trust his or her undivided loyalty. All self-dealing with trust assets is strictly prohibited. The trustee may not favor one class of beneficiaries over another and must diversify the portfolio to avoid unreasonable risk and so on. Moreover, subject to all of these constraints, the trustee's charge is clear: he or she is to maximize the return on trust assets for the benefit of the trust beneficiaries.

By analogy, then, for Christians it is not enough just to declare that we act as God's stewards. It is an important first step but not the end of the discussion. As stewards/trustees we need to know what our goal in managing the "trust corpus" is and what constraints we need to abide by along the way. More specifically, as stewards of God's businesses, we need to know what our goal (or purpose) is when managing the business and what limitations we need to observe to manage the business in accordance with God's desires.[8]

---

[8]In her book *Believers in Business*, Laura Nash describes her findings based on extensive interviews with evangelical business leaders. She notes that the " 'good steward' was the most frequently cited metaphor for personal leadership among the group. For these CEOs it implied service, quality, a responsibility to be fiscally productive and a detachment from self-serving motives" (Laura Nash, *Believers in Business* [Nashville: Thomas Nelson, 1994], p.74).

**3. Human beings are made in the image of God.** On three separate occasions we are told that human beings are made in the image of God.

> Then God said, "Let us make man in our image, in our likeness." . . .
> So God created man in his own image, in the image of God he created
> him; male and female he created them. (Genesis 1:26-27)

What does this mean? In what sense are human beings stamped with God's image?

This is a difficult question to answer and Scripture gives few clues. Theologians have debated the issue at length. The notion that we have been created in God's image is not confined to the Genesis account but is repeated on a number of occasions throughout the Scriptures. Evidently it involves a close parallel between the original and the image; on two occasions—2 Corinthians 4:4; Colossians 1:15—Christ is said to be the "image" of God the Father. It suggests that the image-bearer plays a role in revealing the essence of the Other.

At a minimum, however, we should find in the Genesis use of "image" an intent to reflect those characteristics of God that have already been described in the Genesis account. Specifically, two such characteristics are important for our purpose. First, God has been described as inherently relational ("Let *us* make man in *our* image, in *our* likeness" [Genesis 1:26]). Second, God has been described as a worker. God makes things.

*Relationship.* The God in whose image Adam and Eve were created is the trinitarian God—Father, Son and Holy Spirit—a God inherently relational from before the beginning of time. The plural pronouns in Genesis 1:26 remind us that before God *did* anything, God in three persons *was*. All of the mighty acts of creation flowed out of that relationship. Indeed, because the work of creation was itself an overflowing of the love nature of the Godhead, it was a tangible expression of this relational character. The work gave expression to the relationship. Moreover, since creation was designed to return glory to God, the work of creation not only came out of relationship but was intended to return for the benefit of the Trinity.

As people made in God's image we are reminded that human beings are also inherently relational. We are only fully complete in community. As God remarked about Adam: "It is not good for the man to be alone" (Genesis 2:18). The nurturing and building of community is, therefore, one of the fundamental tasks to be pursued by those seeking to be genuinely human. To be true to the Genesis account, any theology of business must be relational and communitarian in character. Relationships in community must precede labor and productivity. Business must flow from relationship and be shaped so as to flow back to support the community.

*Work*. The God in whose image Adam and Eve were created was also a worker.

> By the seventh day God had finished the *work he had been doing*; so on the seventh day he rested from all his *work*. And God blessed the seventh day and made it holy, because on it he rested from *all the work of creating that he had done*. (Genesis 2:2-3, emphasis added)

Men and women, then, were made in part to work, and by so doing to reflect this aspect of God's glory.

Christians often incorrectly perceive work as having been assigned to human beings as punishment for Adam and Eve's disobedience in the Garden of Eden. Nothing could be further from the truth. The call and the opportunity to work were embedded into the very fabric of human beings as they were first designed by God. Adam and Eve were assigned work in the Garden from the beginning.

And it was not just any work. Since Adam and Eve were created in the image of God, they were made with an inherent capacity for and need to be engaged in creative activity. Of course, their creative activities differed from God's in that only God creates out of nothing *(ex nihilo)*.[9] Human creativity is always derivative, always derived from the work of the Cre-

---

[9]There is no need here to enter into the debate as to whether it is best to characterize human beings as co-creators or subcreators. For our purposes it is sufficient to affirm that to be human is to be intrinsically wired for creative work. See the discussion in Stevens, *Doing God's Business*, p. 24; and Stephen Bretsen, "The Creation, the Kingdom of God, and a Theory of the Faithful Corporation," *Christian Scholar's Review* 38 (2008): 115-54, 138-39. See also John Paul II, *Laborem Exercens*, §§13, 113.

ator. But still, to reflect God's image is to create, to innovate—to bring new things and new ways of doing things into being.

In business terms God made the initial capital investment. He richly endowed the earth with resources. Adam and Eve were the initial managers called to creatively organize (name the animals) and manage these resources (take dominion), to enhance the productivity of the Garden (be fruitful and multiply) in a sustainable (guard creation) manner. Creativity is not just a gift given to some artists or design engineers. It is inherent in the very meaning of being human.

In addition, if the work that Christians do is to reflect the work of God, it must also be meaningful work. After each act of creation, God examined the creative handiwork and pronounced it "good" (Genesis 1:4, 10, 12, 18, 21, 25) and after the creation of human beings, "very good" (v. 31). For our work to mirror God's it too must aim for outcomes that are good. Good work has substance and meaning.

When humans engage in creative, meaningful work that grows out of relationships and gives back to the community they become more deeply human. Of course, work became more difficult as a consequence of the Fall ("Cursed is the ground because of you; . . . it will produce thorns and thistles for you" [Genesis 3:17-18]). But the pre-Fall picture is of human beings gardening and farming on land that readily yielded its produce without demanding payment in sweat and toil. Indeed, pre-Fall work was inherently pleasurable.

One last thought about being made "in the image of God." While there is a sacred quality to all creation—it was all made by God and God pronounced all of it "good"—human beings were given a unique status and dignity. They alone of all the creatures were made "in the image of God" (Genesis 1:27). Down through history the church has consistently taught that the dignity of men and women must be particularly respected in light of their unique place in the created order.

*4. Humans are made to live within limits*. A fourth observation follows from the third. While human beings were made in the image of God, men and women were clearly not made to be gods. Nowhere in the creation narrative are Adam and Eve offered the opportunity to become God, nor are they assured that as originally created, they are already gods. In fact, the narrative takes pains to communicate just the opposite. God preexists. It is God who speaks the world into being, setting its boundaries and defining its essence. God is beyond boundaries. God is unlimited.

By contrast, God places a limit at the very center of human existence.

> In the middle of the garden were the tree of life and the tree of the knowledge of good and evil. . . .
>
> And the LORD God commanded the man, "You are free to eat from any tree in the garden; but you must not eat from the tree of the knowledge of good and evil, for when you eat of it you will surely die." (Genesis 2:9, 16-17)

Thus, to be fully human is to be inherently limited.

The serpent understood this. When the serpent tempted Eve to eat from the forbidden tree, he assured her that by so doing she could be "like God" (Genesis 3:5). The fundamental temptation that Adam and Eve succumbed to was the temptation to deny their limited nature in an effort to be, for themselves, gods.[10]

*5. God delights in variety.* A fifth observation that we can take from the Genesis account is that diversity appears to be built into the very fabric of God's design. Even before God created human beings, God created a wide array of other creatures. Elsewhere in Scripture we are reminded that God enjoys the breadth of creation in all of its variety. It is enjoyed for its own sake and not simply for any utilitarian value that it serves.[11]

When God perceived that Adam was inappropriately "alone," God did not make a second Adam. Rather, God made an Eve. Eve was

---

[10]Of course, this observation has immediate application to business. As I will discuss in much greater detail in chap. 2, many of the consequences of Adam and Eve's unwillingness to accept their limited nature show up in broken aspects of business. Moreover, the institution of business itself is often unwilling to accept a limited role and is tempted instead to exalt itself to God-like status, a consequence that I take up in greater detail in chap. 6.

[11]"'Rejoicing,' 'delighting,' and even, as some translations have it, 'playing' in creation characterize God's involvement in the cosmos" (Loren Wilkinson, "Christ as Creator and Redeemer," in *The Environment and the Christian: What Does the New Testament Say About the Environment?* ed. Calvin B. DeWitt [Grand Rapids: Baker, 1991], p. 35, commenting on Proverbs 8:27-31).

different—a difference that complemented and made whole Adam, who was in himself incomplete.

God's love for diversity is reflected throughout the Scriptures. One of the more confusing passages in the Old Testament relates to an early effort by humanity to build a tower in the city of Babel (Genesis 11:1-9). What marked these efforts was that all those engaged in the building spoke with one language and appeared to be motivated by a single purpose. In this primordial story, God intervenes in judgment, scattering the peoples and giving them a multitude of languages, which precludes them from communicating with one another.

It is often noted that Pentecost was a reversal of God's judgment at Babel, but this is only partially true. It is true in that through the outpouring of the Spirit, unity was once again made possible for God's people. Everyone was able to understand each other and communicate across cultural barriers ("each one heard them speaking in his own language" [Acts 2:6]). It was not a reversal of Babel, however, in the sense that it returned everyone to a single language. Rather, it appears that in God's intended design there will always be a multitude of peoples speaking a multitude of languages. Even at the end of times we are told that kings and nations from around the world, consisting of different peoples and different cultures, will come to worship God (Revelation 21:24). God delights in the diversity of the created order.

**6. The Garden was incomplete.** Finally, in the first two chapters of Genesis humankind is assigned certain tasks. Specifically Adam and Eve were to "subdue" and "rule" over the created order (Genesis 1:28). They were to "be fruitful." In this way they were to "fill the earth" (Genesis 1:28). They were given an opportunity to name the animals, to classify and bring order to creation (Genesis 2:19-20). They were called to "take care of" the earth and thereby protect God's created order (Genesis 2:15). These tasks were given by God to humanity as a blessing. Performance of the tasks allowed men and women to express aspects of their very identities and to delight in the work itself. But the performance of these tasks also served another purpose.

The Garden of Eden before the Fall is correctly described as an expression of God's perfect will. Here the goodness of the original creation prevailed. This goodness was expressed in a flourishing and harmonious peace. It would be incorrect to say, however, that the Garden of Eden as initially created by God was complete—that had Adam and Eve only avoided the forbidden fruit, humankind would have lived to the end of time in this unchanging idyllic garden setting.

In Genesis we are told that after creating the necessary raw materials God still did not cause the fields to flourish because no humans were yet available to work the fields.

> When the Lord God made the earth and the heavens—and no shrub of the field had yet appeared on the earth and no plant of the field had yet sprung up, for the Lord God had not sent rain on the earth *and there was no man to work the ground.* (Genesis 2:4-5, emphasis added)

The Garden was created as a perfectly balanced and resourced starting point. As originally designed, however, the Garden of Eden was not God's intended endpoint. God anticipated moving on from the perfection of the Garden, relying, at least in part, on the activity of the men and women who God had placed in the Garden. They would till the fields. They would gather the fruit. They would understand, organize and classify aspects of the created order. They would create new things. They would be fruitful. As a people they would fill the earth and work the created order to ensure that it was fruitful in a like manner. In other words, God anticipated partnering with human beings to cause the Garden of Eden to flourish.

Of course, God could have chosen to provide for the world supernaturally. Every morning, for example, God could have dropped manna flakes from heaven, and our responsibility would have been limited to running around with our mouths open and our tongues out. But for most of history God did not do this. Rather, human beings were created with a capacity to pool their resources (what we now call "capital"), to design and build an oven (technological innovation), to order and receive shipments of flour (supply chain), to bake bread (operations), to put it on trucks (logistics) and to deliver it to a hungry world. As Martin Luther once said, as we do the work to which we have been called we become the hands of God.[12] We actually take the bread that God intended to provide for a hungry world and make delivery on God's behalf.[13] This work has intrinsic and not just instrumental value in the kingdom of God.

In God's economy, to say that something is perfect is not to suggest that it is done. The Garden was perfect, but it was not static. In fact, even the "end of time" is probably not best conceived of as a static destination where we will someday arrive. As stewards we are not aiming for a fixed endpoint, just for a further and more robust flourishing, an ever-growing and deepening intimacy.[14] At the beginning God didn't deliver a finished product; rather, God provided a setting in which human beings, working with and enabled by God, could cause the created order to flourish.

Thus, to summarize so far, God created the world and everything in it. It belongs to God. As a part of this creation God created men and women and endowed them with a unique dignity. They alone were created in God's image, designed from the beginning to reflect God's glory. They were created for relationship, with one another and with God. They were created as diverse creatures with differences that complemented each other and delighted God. They were called to work as

---

[12]"So we receive our blessings not from them [other human creatures], but from God, through them. Creatures are only the hands, channels, and means through which God bestows all blessings" (Martin Luther, explanation of the First Commandment, "Large Catechism" [1529], in *The Book of Concord,* ed. Theodore Tappert [Philadelphia: Fortress, 1959], p. 368). Luther saw a very close tie between human work and the work of God. "God Himself will milk the cow through him whose calling it is" (quoted in Gordon Preece, "Work," in *The Complete Book of Everyday Christianity,* ed. Robert Banks and R. Paul Stevens [Downers Grove, Ill.: InterVarsity Press, 1997], p. 1126).

[13]"Between 1950 and 2000, grain land productivity climbed by 160 percent while the area planted in grain expanded only 14 percent. This extraordinary rise in productivity, combined with the modest expansion of cultivated area, enabled farmers to triple the grain harvest over the last half-century. At the same time, the growing demand for animal protein was being satisfied largely by a quintupling of the world fish catch to 95 million tons and a doubling of world beef and mutton production, largely from rangelands. These gains not only supported a growth in population from 2.5 billion to 6.1 billion, they also raised food consumption per person, shrinking the share who were hungry" (Lester R. Brown, *Plan B: Rescuing a Planet Under Stress and a Civilization in Trouble* [New York: W. W. Norton, 2003], p. 131.

[14]Isaiah 65:21-22 seems to suggest that work will continue even in the new heavens and the new earth.

co-creators with God, to steward the creation. God intended that men and women would take the raw materials that had been provided and, in partnership with God, help to grow and construct the kingdom here on earth. Men and women were not, however, created to become God. At the center of their existence were to be limits and God called them to live from that place of limitedness.

## GOD'S PURPOSE FOR HUMANKIND:
## NARROWING THE QUESTION

Let us now return to one of the original questions. Does the Westminster Catechism say all that can be said about God's intended role for humankind (to glorify God and enjoy him forever)? Or can we identify a more specific charge to Adam and Eve from the Genesis account?

There is no doubt that the Genesis account confirms that our primary vocation is to glorify God. Created "in his image," our lives are intended to reflect or reveal the divine glory—God's essence and character. But the creation mandate adds specificity to this general calling.

For one, we reflect God's glory through nurturing our relationships with God and with one another. The Garden narrative in Genesis 3 provides us with a tantalizing hint of the intimate friendships that must have existed before the Fall: Adam and Eve walking and chatting with God in the Garden "in the cool of the day" (Genesis 3:8). As we model this loving intimacy in our relationships with God and with others we reflect an aspect of the triune Godhead and give God glory.

But we also glorify God by engaging in the work we have been called to undertake. Already we have seen that this work is to be meaningful, engage our creativity, reflect our diversity, and grow out of and give back to the community. These are characteristics of God's work; when our work reflects these characteristics, we reveal God's glory.

But we have also seen that our work can glorify God in another way. Our work is actually used to accomplish God's purposes on earth. In addition to exhibiting God-like characteristics, we are invited to participate in the bringing about of God-desired results. In Genesis God assigns particular tasks to humanity. Adam and Eve were told to "subdue" and "rule" over the created order, to work the fields, to "multiply" and "be fruitful," to "fill the earth," to give order to creation, and to guard the earth. One aspect of these tasks was to involve Adam and Eve in partnering with God to cause the land to bring forth its crops so as to provide for the material well-being of God's people and the created order. In the performance of these tasks, Adam and Eve advance God's agenda and thereby give God glory. Collectively, these activities enable the community to flourish as God intended. They are to be undertaken for God and, as it is sometimes said, "for the common good."[15]

## THE ROLE OF BUSINESS IN THE CREATION MANDATE

But what does this have to say specifically about business? Business is, of course, not the only institution that human beings operate in. Christians in business are also members of families, citizens of nations, congregants in local churches and participants in various other institutions of civil society (e.g., book clubs, intramural sports teams, food kitchens and environmental groups). What then is the relationship between the work of any one institution and the overall creation mandate?

One possibility, of course, is that each person is called to perform each Genesis task in each institution or role. If this were correct we

---

[15]The notion of the common good has a rich heritage. It shows up in the writings of philosophers down through the ages. It is also one of the central features of Christian, and particularly Catholic, social teaching. In a very simplistic fashion, pursuit of the common good can be understood as making decisions and taking actions that are beneficial to the community as a whole. But as I use the concept in this book I intend a slightly more nuanced understanding. The Catholic religious tradition defines the common good as "the sum of those conditions of social life which allow *social groups* and *their individual members* relatively thorough and ready access to their own fulfillment" (emphasis added). This definition makes clear that it has both an individual and communal element. "Historically, a common good is considered to be a human perfection or fulfillment achievable by a community, such that the community's members all share it, *both as a community and singly*, in their persons. *A common good then, is neither a mere amalgam of private and particular goods nor is it the good of the whole that disregards the good of its members*" (Helen Alford and Michael Naughton, *Managing as If Faith Mattered* [Notre Dame, Ind.: Notre Dame Press, 2001], p. 41, emphasis added). According to the catechism of the Catholic Church, the common good concerns the life of all. It consists of three essential elements. First, it respects the fundamental and inalienable rights of the human person. Specifically, it respects and fosters individual human development. Second, it requires the social well-being and development of the community as a whole. And finally, it requires the peace and stability needed in order to allow for this personal and collective development. Simply put, the common good allows for the flourishing of the community and the individuals who make up that community.

would conclude that *every* Christian in business must *through business* engage in *every* one of the Genesis activities. But surely this cannot be the case. Consider one obvious example. Adam and Eve were called to multiply. That is, they were to enjoy sexual relations and produce offspring. For this "task" there is a corresponding institution, the family. Presumably, during moments of sexual intimacy, neither Adam nor Eve was expected to be tilling the ground or naming animals.

To house the production of offspring in the institution of business (or anywhere else other than in the family) would be a perversion of God's intent. Rather, it would seem that certain institutions are better suited for certain tasks. The family is a better institution in which to situate the bearing and raising of children (be fruitful and multiply). The church and neighborhood might be the best settings to nurture community. Universities may be the best setting for the study and analysis of the created order (naming the animals). The government, with its coercive powers, may be in a better position to assume primary responsibility for guarding creation.

In his letter to the church at Corinth, Paul talks about all of the different functions that the church is to perform. These include teaching, preaching, prophesying, administering and a number of others. But was each individual Christian called to perform all of these functions? Certainly not.

> There are different kinds of service, but the same Lord. There are different kinds of working, but the same God works all of them in all men. Now to each one the manifestation of the Spirit is given for the common good. . . .
>
> The body is a unit, though it is made up of many parts; and though all its parts are many, they form one body. . . .
>
> Now you are the body of Christ, and each one of you is a part of it. And in the church God has appointed first of all apostles, second prophets, third teachers, then workers of miracles, also those having gifts of healing, those able to help others, those with gifts of administration, and those speaking in different kinds of tongues. Are all apostles? Are all prophets? Are all teachers? Do all work miracles? Do all have gifts of

healing? Do all speak in tongues? Do all interpret? (1 Corinthians 12:5-7, 12, 27-30)

In an analogous way, all of humanity is charged with all of the Genesis tasks, but each individual and each individual institution is only one part of the body. Each institution has only a part to play in the whole.

Of course, there is no reason to assume that any given institution will always be responsible for the same aspects of the creation mandate. As the nature of these institutions and the societies they are found in change over time, various aspects of the creation mandate may be reallocated between institutional spheres of activity in different proportions. At some times aspects of the mandate might be best furthered by government action. In different times the same tasks might be best pursued through private enterprise. Sometimes a university should take the lead in advancing research. In other circumstances it might best be conducted by the state or a corporation. A consideration of which tasks make the most sense for which institutions at any given moment is ultimately a time-bound and culturally embedded decision.[16]

So the question boils down to this: In our twenty-first-century context, which aspects of the creation mandate are best suited for business to handle? Or using Paul's language, what is the unique giftedness of business at this time and place in history?

In my judgment, the answer is twofold. First, business appears to be uniquely well situated to work the fields, to cause the land to be fruitful, and to fill the earth—what we might in modern parlance characterize as "to create wealth." Second, business is also the dominant institution (although obviously not the only one) equipped to provide

---

[16]Here I am siding with Nicholas Wolterstorff in his critique of a neo-Calvinists' position that holds that there are certain abiding "types" of social formation—that is that certain institutions are divinely endowed with certain functions in an immutable ontological sense. Wolterstorff argues that "we must ask how the functions performed are best parceled out among the institutions of society: which should be assigned to different institutions, and which to the same. When we look at the various societies to be found in the course of history, we find certain basic functions regularly performed, but we find them parceled out among institutions in all sorts of different ways. Functions that we assign to one institution may in other societies be assigned to different ones. . . . Is our assignment a good one for us? That must be our question" (Nicholas Wolterstorff, *Until Justice and Peace Embrace* [Grand Rapids: Eerdmans, 1983], pp. 62-63).

organized opportunities for meaningful and creative work. With the collapse of the Soviet Union and its state-managed economies, it now appears beyond question that in the twenty-first century private enterprise operating in a relatively free market system will be the institution best positioned to efficiently deliver the goods and services desired by worldwide consumers and the most prolific source of new job creation.

From this I would conclude that at this time in history, there are two legitimate, first-order, intrinsic purposes of business: as stewards of God's creation, business leaders should manage their businesses (1) to provide the community with goods and services that will enable it to flourish, and (2) to provide opportunities for meaningful work that will allow employees to express their God-given creativity. One goal for the Christian businessperson who is stewarding God's business is focused outward—providing goods and services that enhance the quality of life. One goal focuses inward—creating opportunities for individuals within the company to express their vocation in the performance of God-glorifying work.[17] When managers pursue these particular goals for their companies, they participate directly in God's creation mandate. They engage in work of intrinsic and not just instrumental value.[18]

---

[17]"Their view of work is that it has both intrinsic and extrinsic meaning and purpose. That is, the particular work someone does, in and of its own right, is of theological value. Work has the larger role of serving greater societal purposes and needs. Discovering that work can be a calling, and finding meaning and purpose in work are often significant motivators that draw businesspeople to the [Faith at Work] movement" (David Miller, God at Work [New York: Oxford University Press, 2007], p. 135).

[18]From time to time I am challenged to consider a third purpose for business: specifically, that a business exists to "nurture relationships," to "foster community" or words to that effect. And I am almost persuaded. In our twenty-first-century global economy, business does indeed play a central role in community-building. Many employees spend the majority of their waking hours on the job, so their opportunities for nurturing relationships outside of work are limited. Moreover, much of the work that business does depends on individuals working in teams rather than alone. And technology is increasingly enabling teams to gather in virtual spaces so that online relationships can be cultivated in the work place even between individuals who are geographically dispersed. Consistent with the observations drawn from the Genesis creation account I can also readily affirm that the tasks to be undertaken by business must be grounded in community, flow out of community and be designed for the community's common good. Having said this, however, I am ultimately not convinced. If I were asked by a Christian entrepreneur to explain why he should start a new business, it seems sensible and straightforward to explain to him that he should pursue his business because he has a product that can help the world or because he can employ individuals looking for life-giving work. These purposes fit the

Before we press on, let me clarify something about this purpose statement. So far, I have attempted to identify God's purpose for business as a whole. In effect, I have been trying to identify those goals that God might set down were God to write a corporate mission statement for the whole institution of business. I have suggested that the mission statement would focus on the twin goals of providing appropriate goods and services and providing meaningful and creative work. Of course, by negative implication, I have also left some things out. For example, I don't believe that "fostering of relationships in community" or "protecting the environment" would make God's list of fundamental purposes for the institution of business as a whole. This does not mean, however, that these tasks are not essential for human flourishing or even that they are of no importance to business. As we will discuss at length in the following chapters, all faithful businesses will need to take these and a variety of other similar concerns into account—if not as their purpose, their *raison d'être*, then at least as constraints on their operations. We have much more work to do. But we begin with the notion that pursuit of these particular purposes—providing appropriate goods and services, and meaningful and creative work—is a piece of, a starting place for, what it means to be a faithful steward of God's business.

## THREE RELATED OBSERVATIONS

Three closing observations are in order. First, note that this formulation of the purpose of business makes the particular goods and services to be produced a relevant consideration. Specifically, are they goods and services that God would want to make available to the world at this time? Many times I have met with Christians in business who have suggested that the specific output of their efforts is irrelevant. All that counts, they

---

character of business activity. Making products and hiring workers are aspects of a business's DNA. I would also have no problem telling him that his work must in all cases be respectful of relationships and that he should nurture a healthy work community. But this is different than telling him that he should start a business *for the purpose* of nurturing relationships or fostering community. Making community-building a first-order *purpose* of every business stretches the institution of business too far from its fundamental character. This does not mean that healthy work communities are unimportant. They are critical to healthy businesses. They are just not its reason for being; they don't rise to the level of a foundational purpose.

argue, is how they engage in their business activities (e.g., with honesty and compassion). I disagree. Virtually everyone would agree that a pimp or prostitute (even one who does his or her work with integrity, compassion and caring) is unlikely to be furthering the kingdom of God through these professions. A full understanding of the creation mandate should extend this further. In certain times and places, faithful obedience to God's kingdom values might require that we invest less of our aggregate capital in the production of violent video games and more in the development of sanitary water facilities for developing countries, less in weapons of mass destruction and more in quality wood products, less in fossil fuels and more in renewable resources.

Under the business model that operates in most corporations today, deciding which product should be produced comes down to assessing which of the products that the company could produce would yield the highest return on investment (ROI). While this is not always easy to calculate (and is often calculated incorrectly), it has the seductive quality of mathematical certainty.[19] It does not, however, necessarily lead to operations that accord with kingdom values. Online betting and pornography may yield higher rates of return but are unlikely to lead to human flourishing.

Of course, it is not possible to come up with a particular formula that will clearly dictate which goods or services should be produced. There is no single litmus test. Each of us faithfully listening to God may come

---

[19]Al Erisman, long-time head of research and development in technology and mathematics for the Boeing Company, has argued that while the promise is seductive, achieving this certainty is often not even mathematically possible: "The second thing we learn from optimization is that these problems are very difficult. No one really knows how to truly solve most nonlinear, time-dependent mathematical optimization problems (which is the nature of the problem as formulated). So we do in practice what any good mathematician would do—we approximate the problem by something we can solve. In practice, what this means is that while it is very difficult to maximize shareholder value subject to constraints over the long term, we can likely be more effective in doing this over the short term. The pressures from Wall Street for short-term results only support the solution to this problem rather than the stated problem. It is generally not the case that a sequence of best solutions for the short term will together lead to the best solution in the long term. Anyone hiking in the mountains knows that to get to the peak you sometimes have to move lower before climbing higher. Similarly, short-term thinking in business may look good at the moment, but it often has very significant longer-term issues" (Al Erisman, "The New Capitalism?" *Ethix* 66 [2009]: 4-5).

up with a different answer. But even if we may end up with different answers, we are called to start by asking a common question: Instead of asking in the first instance, *Which choice will maximize my ROI?* we ask instead, *Given the core competencies of my organization and the assets under its control, how can I best direct the organization to serve? Which products or services could we produce that would best enable my community to flourish?*

And this leads to a second observation. Note that nothing in this Genesis model supports the conclusion that business should be operated for the purpose of maximizing profits. In fact, this model turns the dominant business model on its head. In most business schools today and in most corporations (particularly larger, publicly traded corporations) the sole legitimate purpose of business is said to be maximizing profits for the sake of the shareholders.[20] Indeed, influential

---

[20]Setting my proposed Genesis-stewardship model against the shareholder-maximization model presents the most dramatic contrast. Of course, the shareholder-maximization model is not the only existing option for describing the duty of a corporate manager (and the corresponding purpose of the firm). Since the publication of R. Edward Freeman's seminal work *Strategic Management: A Stakeholder Approach* (Boston: Pitman, 1984) a competing approach to understanding management's responsibilities has been advanced under the heading of "stakeholder theory." There have been almost as many definitions of this theory as there have been articles written about it, but in general terms this theory assumes that management owes duties not just to shareholders but to other constituent groups that have a stake in the company, typically including at least employees, customers and suppliers. While this is an overly simplistic statement, in general this theoretical approach calls on management to make decisions in the interests of all stakeholders and to balance competing interests (in one fashion or another). As such this theory would certainly allow for a consideration of the business purposes that I am advocating, although this theory is not without its own theological shortcomings (see Alford and Naughton, *Managing as If Faith Mattered*, pp. 55-60).

There is no doubt that the stakeholder theory has gained in acceptance since it was first introduced, although the extent of its adoption in practice is difficult to assess for several reasons. First, management focused simply on increasing shareholder wealth may nonetheless adopt policies and make pronouncements that outwardly appear to be focused on other constituencies. For example, a company might adopt employee-friendly strategies ostensibly to respond to legitimate employee desires but actually do so because it desires to reduce turnover, lower costs and enhance profits. Conversely, management actually operating under a stakeholder framework may nonetheless choose to justify its actions as a means of maximizing shareholder wealth. Management might engage in this obfuscation because claiming benefits for shareholders would allow management to invoke the "business judgment" rule and reduce the chance that it might be the subject of lawsuits alleging violations of its fiduciary duties. Complicating matters further, most articles written about stakeholder theory are theoretical rather than empirical in nature and are tipped heavily (and disproportionately) in the direction of large public companies (André O. Laplume, Karan Sonpar and Reginald A. Litz, "Stakeholder Theory: Reviewing a Theory That Moves Us," *Journal of Management* 34 [2008]: 1152-

economists have argued that business managers have a moral obligation to do everything within their power (short of breaking the law and violating conventional norms of society) to maximize profits.[21] Under this model, providing meaningful work to employees and being honest and straightforward with customers are good business practices *to the extent, and only to the extent*, that they enhance the bottom line. In other words employees and customers become a means for achieving the goal of maximizing shareholder wealth.

Under the Genesis model, however, the employees and customers become the actual ends of the business. The business is run for their welfare. Profit is not important as an end in and of itself. Rather, it becomes the means of attracting sufficient capital to allow the business to do what, from God's perspective, it is in business to do—that is, to serve its customers and employees.

Of course, this doesn't mean that profit is unimportant. Generating profits is critical. "No margin, no mission." Without profit a business dies. But the Genesis model places profit in a proper perspective. It becomes the means to service rather than the purpose of the enterprise itself.[22]

> To turn shareholders' needs into a purpose is to be guilty of a logical confusion, to mistake a necessary condition for a sufficient one. We need to eat to live; food is a necessary condition of life. But if we lived mainly to eat, making food a sufficient or sole purpose of life, we would become gross. The purpose of a business, in other words, is not to make a profit, full stop. It is to make a profit so that the business can do something more or better.[23]

And one last observation. Sometimes I worry that to suggest that one of the fundamental purposes of business is to "produce goods and

---

89, 1160, 1172). In short, it is simply hard to tell how much ground the stakeholder theory has actually gained on the shareholder maximizing model.

[21]See, e.g., Milton Friedman, "The Social Responsibility of Business Is to Increase Its Profits," *New York Times Magazine*, September 13, 1970, pp. 122-26.

[22]Chapter 8 contains an in-depth discussion of the importance and role of profit in a company operating under the Genesis model of business purpose which I advocate for in this chapter.

[23]Charles Handy, "What's a Business For?" *Harvard Business Review* 80, no. 12 (2002): 51.

services that enable the community to flourish" might conjure up some image of a cookie-cutter manufacturing process whereby the same goods are just repetitively stamped out by machines year after year and handed out to customers who come by. But this would be a mistake.

I intend a far more robust understanding. Indeed the Genesis model statement of purpose assigns a very high calling to business. Business is to be in the business of "value creation" or "creating wealth." Put simply, successful businesses find ways through innovation to *make more or better things from less*. In so doing, business generates the economic capital that sustains the entire society.

> At the very heart of capitalism . . . is the creative habit of enterprise. Enterprise is, in its first moment, the inclination to notice, the habit of discerning, the tendency to discover what other people don't yet see. It is also the capacity to act on insight, so as to bring into reality things not before seen. It is the ability to foresee both the needs of others and the combinations of productive factors most adapted to satisfying those needs. This habit of intellect constitutes an important source of wealth in modern society. Organizing such a productive effort, planning its duration in time, making sure that it corresponds in a positive way to the demands it must satisfy, and taking the necessary risks: all this has been a source of new wealth in the past 200 years.[24]

As Bonnie Wurzbacher, a senior vice president with Coca Cola put it in a recent interview, "As the sole source of wealth creation in the world, [business] enables every other social, civic and even spiritual institutions [*sic*] to exist."[25] In economic terms, all other institutions are funded (through taxes or philanthropic giving) by the wealth first created by business. This can be seen when a new business moves into a community, and is often felt acutely when a business closes or departs.

The call "to produce goods and services that enable flourishing" is a call to participate in this innovative and industrious work. It is a call to constantly be looking for ways to deliver more or better goods and ser-

---

[24]Michael Novak, *Business as a Calling* (New York: Free Press, 1996), p. 120.
[25]Telephone interview with Bonnie Wurzbacher reported on *Worldview Matters*, October 9, 2009 <http://biblicalworldviewmatters.blogspot.com/search/label/Bonnie%20Wurzbacher>.

vices. In fact, it is the combination of the two purposes I have identified previously—enabling creative work (innovation) and producing community-flourishing products (productivity)—that really brings businesses' unique contribution into sharpest focus.

## CONCLUSION

Let's finish the parable we started with. What can we tell our student considering a career in business? In short, we can tell her that she is considering a noble calling that will involve her in delivering on key aspects of God's creation mandate. If a Christian lawyer seeks to advance God's justice, and a Christian doctor seeks to administer God's healing, a Christian businessperson seeks to serve a hurting world by providing it with the material goods and services that will enable it to prosper. The Christian in business enables individuals to express aspects of their God-given identities by affording them the opportunity to participate in meaningful and creative work. In short, the Christian in business is in the business of rendering service that will enable humanity to flourish.

## 2

# Broken

How could something that started out so good end up going so bad?

## GOOD GOES BAD

*Dumping in India.* In June 1999 a large multinational company established a factory on a thirty-one-acre plot in India and began to manufacture over five hundred thousand liters of bottled drinks per day. As part of the manufacturing process, the factory (in compliance with local laws) dumped substantial volumes of sludge containing large quantities of heavy metals near a local aquifer. Shortly after the operations of the plant had begun, local residents noticed a deterioration of their water quality and began to report various health problems, including abdominal discomfort, drowsiness, convulsions, fatigue, headaches, and itching in limbs. Cases of developmental disabilities, bleeding from noses, and patches on skin in children were noticed. Women saw a rise in spontaneous abortions and stillbirths. Certain crop yields in the area decreased by fifty percent. The plant was closed in 2004, but two years later there still had been no noticeable improvement in the water quality, crop fecundity or health of the nearby villagers.[1]

*Sweatshops in Nicaragua.* Encouraged by various tax incentives, a

---

[1]"Ground Water Resources in Plachimada," Hazards Centre, New Delhi, and People's Science Institute, Dehradun, June 2006 <www.IndiaResource.org/documents/PlachimadaReportWater Pollution.pdf>.

number of foreign companies have established manufacturing facilities in Nicaragua's Zona Franca (free trade zone). The factories operate behind fences in an area located on the outskirts of Managua and provide forty thousand jobs in a country where unemployment runs as high as 60 percent.[2] Working conditions, however, are oppressive. Wages fall well short of "livable wages" and are further reduced through various gimmicks. For example, when a couple of days are missed due to illness, pay for the entire week will often be docked. Workers are routinely required to perform overtime work without advance notice. The working environment involves long lines of workers in extremely hot and sometimes very loud conditions. It is not at all unusual for workers to faint on the job. Employees are not allowed to talk to each other, nor are they allowed to have water or food at their station. Permission must be requested for bathroom breaks, which are limited to three minutes. As workers leave each day, they are routinely frisked and sporadically strip searched.

The employees are nearly all women in their late teens and early twenties. The companies select young women because they are least likely to try to organize for worker rights and are the most desirable for male managers seeking to "hit on" female employees. Violent and sexually abusive bosses appear to be common. Notwithstanding the terrible working conditions, however, the employees routinely stay on the jobs as long as possible. Every morning there is a small crowd of young women standing outside the factory gates hoping to be hired. Any employee who creates a problem can be easily replaced.[3]

***Enron convictions and the collapse of the company.*** Within months of being hailed as the "industry standard for excellence," "the one to emulate" and "one of the world's most innovative companies," Enron filed for bankruptcy. Four thousand workers were laid off. Longtime Enron employees lost not only critical health benefits but hundreds of thou-

---

[2]Filadelfo Aleman, "Nicaragua Firings Cast a Harsh Spotlight," *Seattle Times*, February 20, 2001, sec. A 6.

[3]Based on my interviews of women who worked in a Nicaragua free trade zone, February 2001, Managua, Nicaragua.

sands of dollars as the value of Enron stock in their pension plans collapsed during a period when they were not allowed to sell. Other shareholders and lenders likewise lost billions in investment dollars. The economic consequences spilled out across Houston, across other energy companies and eventually across all of corporate America. One of the five largest accounting firms in the world collapsed in its wake.

In retrospect it appears that much of the touted value of Enron (and much of the spectacular rise in its stock price) had been made up and sustained through a complicated construct of smoke and mirrors intentionally developed to mask losses and obscure huge worthless investments, with the complicity of a number of major investment houses and banks. Safeguard groups, including rating agencies, government agencies, analysts and others, failed to alert the public. All the while, some of the senior leaders of Enron were personally pocketing tens of millions of dollars in side deals and secretive stock sales. Ken Lay and Jeffrey Skilling, the chief executives who guided Enron through its spectacular rise and fall, were later found guilty of fraud, conspiracy and, in the case of Skilling, insider trading. Ken Lay died from a heart attack while his conviction was on appeal.[4]

***Child labor in Chinese kiln factories.*** In Henan and Shanxi provinces in China, children as young as eight years old were kidnapped and forced to work as slaves in illegal brick kiln factories and coal mines. Initially, local authorities looked the other way, but once the abductions were brought to light by coalitions of parents searching for their children, the government began investigating. State television conservatively estimated that at least one thousand minors had been tricked into and trapped in this work. The children were fed little and frequently forced to work as much as eighteen hours a day. The owners of the operations ran them like prisons, using fierce dogs and thugs who beat the

---

[4]The saga of Enron and its collapse has been widely documented in books and the popular press. See, for example, Mimi Swartz and Sherron Watkins, *Power Failure: The Inside Story of the Collapse of Enron* (New York: Doubleday, 2003); Bethany McLean and Peter Elkind, *The Smartest Guys in the Room: The Amazing Rise and Scandalous Fall of Enron* (New York: Penguin, 2004); and Kurt Eichenwald, *Conspiracy of Fools: A True Story* (New York: Broadway Books, 2005). As of this writing, Skilling's conviction is on appeal.

children at will. One mine owner reportedly beat a child worker to death with a shovel. Children who were rescued were found emaciated and covered with wounds.[5]

***Racism at Texaco.*** In the mid-1990s, six employees filed a class-action suit against Texaco on behalf of fifteen hundred salaried African Americans. The suit alleged pervasive patterns of discrimination in promotion and pay. According to one survey, relative to other companies in the same industry, Texaco had a below-average percentage of blacks in every salary bracket over $50,000. Promotions of black employees were delayed by years relative to their white counterparts. Evaluations were skewed. For example, in the accounting division, approximately 50 of 142 employees had been assigned one of the top two evaluation ratings. Only one of the 50, however, was a minority-group employee. In some instances key promotions were made from a secret "high-potential employee" list. In 1994, of the 178 names on that list, only 6 were names of black employees. The lawsuit also alleged numerous incidents of discriminatory and humiliating treatment aimed at individual minority employees.

As might be expected, Texaco vigorously contested the lawsuit for over two-and-a-half years. Then, on November 4, 1996, the *New York Times* printed an article revealing the contents of a secret tape recording made of a conversation between senior executives of the company. The recordings revealed plans to destroy evidence that had been sought in the lawsuit. More damning, however, were the derogatory comments heard being made by the Texaco executives. Black employees were referred to as "niggers" and "black jelly beans." "This diversity thing, you know how all the black jelly beans agree," noted one executive. "That's funny," replied another, "All the black jelly beans seem to be glued to the bottom of the bag."

The public reaction was immediate and intense. Nationwide boycotts of Texaco products were proposed. Shareholders expressed outrage. The CEO apologized and within ten days, the company agreed to

---

[5]"Child Brickwork Slave Children May Number 1,000," *Reuters AlertNet*, June 15, 2007 <www.alertnet.org/thenews/newsdesk/PEK228447.htm>; Howard W. French, "Beijing's Lack of Penalties in Labor Cases Stir Outrage," *New York Times*, July 17, 2007, sec. A8; Howard W. French, "Reports of Forced Labor at Brick Kilns Unsettle China," *New York Times*, June 16, 2007, sec. A3.

settle the lawsuit. The settlement required Texaco to pay more than $140 million. In addition, Texaco agreed to change the way it administered its personnel operations (including turning over authority for such operations to a committee largely appointed by outsiders) at an estimated additional cost of $35 million.[6]

*Joe Camel advertising.* R. J. Reynolds (RJR) first adopted the Joe Camel symbol in 1913 to go with its Camel cigarettes. In the late 1980s RJR revived the symbol with a new "cartoon" look. The new Joe Camel came complete with an aviator jacket (á la Top Gun), sunglasses and a smirk. After introducing the new symbol, Camel's shipments rose 11.3 percent. More significantly, since the reintroduction of Joe Camel, Camel's share of the under-eighteen market climbed to 33 percent from 5 percent. This was not surprising. The *Journal of the American Medical Association* published three surveys that found that the cartoon character Joe Camel was a very effective way to reach children. Over half of children between the ages of three and six recognized Joe Camel and associated him with Camel cigarettes. Six-year-olds were as familiar with Joe Camel as they were with Mickey Mouse. Over 97 percent of teenagers had seen "old Joe." Nearly 60 percent thought that the ads he was in were "cool." Camel was identified by 33 percent of the students who smoked as their favorite brand. It has been shown that lifetime addiction to cigarettes is inaugurated most effectively in the young, and consequently youth smoking has the most potential for serious health effects over a lifetime. When the American Medical Association asked RJR to pull its ads, it initially refused. In 1997, however, RJR agreed to discontinue use of the cartoon character in settlement of a lawsuit that was challenging its practices as targeting underage smokers. RJR continues to deny that Camel sales were really aimed at youth.[7]

---

[6]Kurt Eichenwald, "Texaco to Make Record Payout in Bias Lawsuit," *New York Times*, November 16, 1996, 1.1; Kurt Eichenwald, "The Two Faces of Texaco," *New York Times*, November 10, 1996, 3.1; Kurt Eichenwald, "Texaco Executives, On Tape, Discussed Impeding a Bias Suit," *New York Times*, November 4, 1996, sec. A1.

[7]Marianne M. Jennings, "Joe Camel: The Cartoon Character Who Sells Cigarettes," in *Ethical Issues in Business: A Philosophical Approach*, ed. Thomas Donaldson and Patricia Werhane, 6th ed. (Upper Saddle River, N.J.: Prentice Hall, 1999), pp. 446-48.

***Ford Motor Pinto crashes.*** In August of 1970, Ford Motor Company deliberately released the Pinto to production while knowing that its fuel tank was a serious fire hazard. Based on the design of the vehicle, a rear-end collision could easily rupture the Pinto's fuel system and cause horrific fires. For more than eight years after the initial release of the vehicle, however, Ford resisted changes in government safety standards that would have required it to fix the fire-prone gas tanks. This resistance continued notwithstanding that Pinto crashes caused between five hundred and nine hundred burn deaths during this period. The reason for all of this: the application of a cost-benefit analysis. In 1972, the National Highway Traffic Safety Administration calculated that the value of a human life was $200,725. Using a cost-benefit analysis and assuming that it would be required to pay damages in the case of burn injuries, Ford estimated that the total expenses it would incur without the fix would amount to slightly under $50 million. According to Ford's records the problem with the gas tank could be fixed at a price of $11 per vehicle. Extending this cost over the number of cars that Ford anticipated selling would amount to a $137 million cost. Ford concluded that it was cheaper to continue to manufacture the fire-prone cars and pay damages when drivers were burned to death than to make the $11 fix.[8]

## WHAT WENT WRONG?

In light of God's good design, how could we end up with examples like these? Business was intended to enable human flourishing not destroy it. What happened? What went wrong?

As originally created, the Garden of Eden was a perfectly resourced environment. God pronounced it "very good." It was characterized by a constellation of harmonious relationships and a deep enjoyment. The Garden was filled with a rich, satisfying and balanced peace. Adam

---

[8]This Ford decision has been a standard case study in business ethics texts. See, for example, Manuel G. Velasquez, *Business Ethics; Concepts and Cases*, 5th ed. (Upper Saddle River, N.J.: Prentice Hall, 2002), pp. 73-75. Ford's decision was originally brought to light in a Mother Jones investigative report (Mark Dowie, "Pinto Madness," *Mother Jones*, September-October 1977, pp. 18-32).

and Eve's relationship with God was easy. Their relationships with each other and with the rest of the created order were in balance. Work had a role in the Garden, but it was a role balanced by walks with God and other leisure activities. Although this word is never used in the creation account itself, perhaps one of the best ways to characterize the Garden is to note that it was a place fully infused with God's *shalom*.[9]

Of course, the goodness and balance of the Garden depended in part on the maintenance of certain limits. For Adam and Eve these implicit limits crystallized in a single command: They were not to eat of the tree of the knowledge of good and evil. They were to accept that God alone was without limits. Everything depended on their keeping this command. It was the lynch pin of the Garden. If this command were respected, the Garden would hold together and remain in shalom.

Tragically, however, this was not to be.

> When the woman saw that the fruit of the tree was good for food and pleasing to the eye, and also desirable for gaining wisdom, she took some and ate it. She also gave some to her husband, who was with her, and he ate it. (Genesis 3:6)

By disobeying God and eating of the tree of the knowledge of good and evil, Adam and Eve asserted their unwillingness to live within limits (or to be less than God). This is what theologians refer to as the Fall. Not only did this disrupt their relationships with God but it tore a hole through the whole fabric of the "good" creation. Nothing has been the same ever since.

Genesis 3 outlines the consequences of Adam and Eve's disobedience. Immediately, the easy relationship between God and Adam was

---

[9] *Shalom* is first used in Genesis 15:15 and is often translated in English as "peace" or "welfare." It is part of the promise found in the law (Leviticus 26:6). It finds its fullest expression, however, in the poetic and prophetic literature, particularly in the Psalms and in the writings of Isaiah. Nicholas Wolterstorff describes the concept at length: "Shalom is the human being dwelling at peace in all his or her relationships: with God, with self, with fellows, with nature. . . . But the peace which is shalom is not merely the absence of hostility, not merely being in right relationship. Shalom at its highest is enjoyment in one's relationships. . . . To dwell in shalom is to enjoy living before God, to enjoy living in one's physical surroundings, to enjoy living with one's fellows, to enjoy life with oneself" (Nicholas Wolterstorff, *Until Justice and Peace Embrace* [Grand Rapids: Eerdmans, 1983], pp. 69-70).

disrupted. Rather than walking with God in the Garden, Adam hid. Whereas previously Adam and Eve had been happy to rely on God's provisions, now they made their first set of clothes.

Similarly, the relationship between Adam and Eve was disrupted. Previously, they had lived in easy intimacy with one another. Now, aware of their own nakedness, they sought to hide. When questioned by God, Adam turned on Eve. Later in the chapter, Adam named Eve (an assertion of hierarchy and authority previously reserved only for Adam's relationship with the animals).

Nature itself was cursed. Thorns and thistles now grew where crops previously flourished. Fruitfulness (and the fulfillment of the creation mandate) now became painful. For Eve, it was to be pain in childbirth; for Adam, it was in the sweat of his brow as he worked the land. In short, shalom was upended.

Business today operates after the Fall, and this is critical to our development of a theology of business. It would be worse than naive to think that all that we need to do is to realign our purpose for business with the creation mandate and try harder. Everything is broken and a far deeper fix is needed.

## CONSEQUENCES OF BROKEN GOD-HUMAN RELATIONS FOR BUSINESS

The first-order breach is the rupture of the relationship between God, on the one hand, and men and women, on the other. When Adam and Eve ate the fruit, it was, before anything else, a rejection of God. Everything flows from this reality.

This broken relation manifests itself in many ways in business. Perhaps most significantly, men and women in business have often lost a sense of meaning about their work. In the Garden work was situated in the context of humankind's partnership with God, and this relationship gave meaning and direction to the work. Work, in effect, was to be God-centered.

With the Fall, however, death became an inevitable reality—"the wages of sin is death" (Romans 6:23). Fear of death became the operating motif, and work, rather than being a joyful expression of one aspect of the God-human relationship, became a means of self-protection and preservation. Rather than being a peaceful, God-centered activity, it became, at base, a human-focused project designed at its deepest level to hold death at bay. Thus the original meaning of work was seriously distorted.

Some have attempted to fill a hollow sense of purpose by locating meaning in career advancement or in the size of compensation packages. Others have looked for meaning in their ability to be productive and to continue to earn a paycheck. Still others have attempted to find meaning in their enjoyment of particular job activities. One symptom of these alternate, and ultimately inadequate, sources of meaning, however, is the difficulty that many encounter upon retirement. Depression and a sense of loss of purpose is a common phenomenon among recent retirees. Moreover, even during their work lives, many are plagued with the "Is this all there is?" question. As Bob Buford, a highly successful cable TV entrepreneur and author of *Halftime*, described his own experience, "There was something gnawing at me. How was it that I could be so successful, so fortunate, and yet so frustratingly unfulfilled?"[10]

At a deep level the disruption of relations with God has also produced an identity crisis. Even as many of us search for a deeper sense of meaning in our work, work has become our identity. Increasingly, many of us know ourselves primarily in terms of what we produce. "We are what we do."[11] This, of course, is exactly the opposite of what God intended. From the divine perspective our identity is wrapped up in the fact that we have been made "in God's image" and are God's beloved children. It is only out of this identity that we are called to work. "We are to do what we are."[12] Paradoxically, even as work seems to have less and less meaning for many of us, it plays a greater and greater role in fashioning our perceptions of who we are.

---

[10]Bob Buford, *Halftime* (Grand Rapids: Zondervan, 1994), pp. 33-34.
[11]This notion is discussed in the context of vocation by Os Guinness in his book *The Call* (Nashville: Word, 1998), pp. 44-54.
[12]Ibid.

The loss of intimacy with God also impairs discernment. The shift from a God-centered to a me-centered approach often leads to distorted judgments. For example, a number of the high-profile actors in the recent spate of corporate frauds were active churchgoers and, on some occasions, very outspoken about their faith. It appears, however, that many of them got caught up in corporate cultures where the overarching goal of enhancing stock price or shareholder value began to blind to them to ethical considerations. They invested so much of their attention to spinning their earnings that they became dizzy and lost their way.

Even those who faithfully continue to seek after God and ask for the Spirit's guidance in business decisions find that correctly discerning God's will is far more challenging after the Fall. Very few Christians experience the equivalent of regular afternoon walks in the Garden with God. For most, discerning God's will now involves a murky process of reading Scripture, praying, seeking advice from fellow Christians, watching circumstances unfold, applying principles and trusting that God is at work redeeming even bad decisions. It is striking how few Christian business-ethics texts recommend simply prayerfully asking God what to do when faced with ethical dilemmas. Instead, these texts teach the need for a careful consideration of all relevant factors, identification of ethical principles, application of these principles and so on. In short, these textbooks suggest that most of time the godly, ethical choice is up to us to figure out. And if they perhaps sell short the possibility of more moment-by-moment assistance from God and the enabling work of the Holy Spirit, they nonetheless correctly reflect the reality that the Fall has made it much more difficult to hear what God is saying.

## CONSEQUENCES OF BROKEN HUMAN-HUMAN RELATIONS FOR BUSINESS

The Fall also ripped a hole in God's desire for relations between people. Adam and Eve began to focus on themselves and sought to hide from the community. They became adversarial. Hierarchy and dominance ("your husband will rule over you") replaced the model of cooperation.

These features continue to find expression in many aspects of business relations today. Without suggesting that the following is at all comprehensive, consider some of the following arenas where tension has replaced the harmony and peace that God intended.

***Disruption in organizational relationships.*** Anyone who has ever worked with anyone else will need little convincing about the broken nature of regular interactions in the workplace. Office politics, malicious gossip, behind-the-back criticisms, cliques, truth "spinning," destructive personal ambitions, free-riding, domineering behavior, sexism, racism, jealousy, self-promotion—these are all common features of today's corporate environments. And even where enlightened management is able to largely avoid these symptoms of brokenness, there are always the more subtle failures: the failure to listen well, the unintended but nonetheless hurtful comment, the insensitivity to the burdens of others and so on. The truth of the matter is that in our everyday, ordinary encounters we often don't relate to our coworkers all that well. The Fall is at work.

***Livable wages.*** Business managers often treat employees without the dignity due those made in the image of God. For example, many jobs fail to pay a livable wage. The concept of a livable wage has been defined in various ways, but at its essence it is a wage that is sufficient to enable the wage earner (and where applicable, the family he or she supports) to meet basic needs, or as Michael Naughton describes it, "a living wage . . . is the minimum amount due to every independent wage earner by the mere fact that he is a human being with a life to maintain and a personality to develop."[13] An employer must recognize that the full-time employment of an individual uses up that individual's earning capacity. If it does not yield enough for the employee to live on, it violates the personhood of that individual as designed by God.

We can certainly debate what package of goods should be included as basic needs, but when the issue is dignity, a possible starting point might be one aspect of Nobel Prize winner Amartya Sen's capabilities-

---

[13]Michael Naughton, "A Theology of Fair Pay," *Regent Business Review* 15 (2005): 9, 11.

based definition of poverty: not having enough to appear in public or participate in the life of the community without shame.[14] In our American culture some have suggested that this leads to the conclusion that basic needs include at least food, housing, child care, transportation, health care, clothing, household and personal expenses, insurance, and amounts necessary for the payment of required taxes. Although the precise calculation of a livable wage depends on the region and the chosen bundle of goods, and although the applicable minimum wage in the United States varies by state, in many jurisdictions, the minimum wage is only about one half of the corresponding livable wage.[15]

*Unsafe working conditions.* In many parts of the world employees are asked to work in inherently dangerous and unhealthy work settings. Often employees will accept these jobs because no meaningful alternatives are available to them. There have been many instances of workers handling toxic materials without adequate training and protection. Some textile workers have been required to work long hours in factories without adequate ventilation. Mining employees have been required to work without needed safety equipment. Others have been forced to work in settings with inadequate sanitation.

Moreover, in addition to physical dangers, work places can often be rendered unhealthy by dehumanizing and abusive policies. For example, in many settings the willingness to perform sexual favors for supervisors is made an implicit condition of continued employment. As noted in the discussion of Nicaragua's free trade zones, some employers have precluded coworkers from talking to one another while they work for fear of encouraging concerted employee action. Others require permission to use the bathroom or subject employees to strip searches. In all

---

[14]Amartya Sen, "The Political Economy of Targeting," in *Public Spending and the Poor*, ed. Dominique van de Walle and Kimberly Nead (Washington, D.C.: John Hopkins University Press, 1995), p. 15.

[15]One tool available for calculating a livable wage is the Livable Wage Calculator developed by Amy Glasmeier, professor of geography and regional planning at Penn State University. The calculator, found at www.livingwage.geog.psu.edu, draws on various federal sources of information to compile its calculations. This calculator allows us to calculate a living wage by locale for families of different sizes. The statement in the text assumes that a living wage should be calculated for a single adult with one child—although that of course is debatable.

of these cases, and sadly in many others, the conditions of employment denigrate the individual and fail to treat him or her as one made in the image of God.

***Employee privacy.*** The ability to function as an autonomous individual requires some measure of privacy. The ability to control the dissemination of some personal information about oneself is a critical component of what it means to be a human being. At the same time, in business, individual employees function as part of a community. Preservation and protection of the community and the advancement of its collective business goals may, in many cases, be enhanced by diminishing the scope of any one individual employee's privacy.

For example, most businesses today monitor employees' use of email on company machines during company time. While most employers are willing to allow a modest level of personal use of such email, they typically reserve the right to ensure that the email does not violate community norms regarding offensive speech and is not being used to steal company trade secrets. Similar policies are often found to ensure that employees are not engaged in inappropriate use of the Internet. Many ethicists would accept this level of "privacy invasion" as a reasonable quid pro quo for continued employment.

But where are the appropriate lines? What if an employer does not notify employees in advance that it will be monitoring email and Internet use? What if a manager continues reading what is a clearly a private email that does not raise any legitimate business concerns? Does that cross the line? Should employers be able to use keystroke technology (technology that records and saves each keystroke) to reconstruct the text of emails an employee drafts but later elects to delete without sending? Is this an appropriate level of protection of business interests, or is this a violation of the employee's internal thought processes? Can employers legitimately make use of surveillance cameras? With or without notice to employees? What about hidden cameras in bathrooms or locker rooms where employees change into company uniforms? Do unannounced random drug tests violate an employee's right to control the dissemination of his or her personal information?

Again, while different people may draw lines in different places, the tension inherent in these issues is at odds with the harmony of the Garden. Moreover, it is clear that there have been many instances where the advancement of business interests has crossed the line and violated individual autonomy.

*Advertising aimed at children.* Kids have become a primary object of advertiser attention. They are ripe targets. For example, based on a 1999 study, the average child between ages two and seven spent more than three and a half hours every day using media of some sort. In general, kids spend between nineteen and twenty hours every week watching television. The average child in America grows up in a home with three television sets. More than three-fourths of sixth-graders have a TV in their own bedroom.[16]

In the words of sociologist Amitai Etzioni, "children begin life as highly vulnerable and dependent persons, unable to make reasonable choices on their own, and gradually grow to become . . . people able to make moral judgments, competent to act on their own, and ready to be autonomous persons."[17] Notwithstanding this vulnerability and the strong opposition of the American Academy of Pediatrics (AAP) to marketing products through "programming that targets children younger than age 2," however, ads target very young children with ever greater accuracy. Douglas Rushkoff, a media critic notes that "today the most intensely targeted demographic is the baby—the future consumer. . . . The fresh neurons of young brains are valuable mental real estate to admen."[18]

The efforts of the advertising community to access particularly the "young kid" market have been documented in a report, "Watch Out for

---

[16]"Fact Sheet," Kaiser Family Foundation <www.kff.org/entmedia/upload/Kids-Media-The-New-Millennium-Fact-Sheet.pdf> based on data from the Kaiser Family Foundation study, *Kids and Media @ The New Millennium, November 1999;* and J. Lyle and H. Hoffman, "Children's Use of Television and Other Media," in *Television and Social Behavior,* vol. 4, ed. E. A. Rubinstein, G. A. Comstock, and J. Murray (Washington, D.C.: U.S. Government Printing Office, 1972), p. 140.

[17]Amitai Etzioni, *The Monochrome Society* (Princeton, N.J.: Princeton University Press, 2001), p. 108.

[18]Douglas Rushkoff, *Coercion: Why We Listen to What "They" Say* (New York: Riverhead Books, 1999), p. 176.

Children: A Mothers' Statement to Advertisers," from the Motherhood Project, 2001.[19] The report describes industry conferences attended by leading advertising, marketing and programming executives where the goal is "to create brand loyalty at an early age that will be remembered for generations."[20] Research findings and case studies focusing on the birth-to-three age group were presented. One workshop provided "hands-on training" in the latest trend in effective toddler and youth research: anthropological research, and the use of "observational research techniques" to help marketers "find out the desires of toddler-age consumers."[21]

In the words of *Kidscreen:*

> Progressive agencies meet with kids on a regular basis to find out the relevant brand insight for new products and concepts. Beyond traditional focus groups, methods employed include "friendship pairs," in which kids talk to each other about products; . . . playlabs, to observe kids' play patterns with products; and . . . CAPS (Child and Parents Studies), . . . which evaluate the "nag factor" (the influence kids have in purchasing a product) by determining if the information communicated to a child enables them to convince the parent to make a purchase.
>
> Through the use of increasingly sophisticated behavioral science studies and techniques set forth in expensive and well-researched industry papers such as "The Nag Factor" and "The Art of Fine Whining," you encourage our children to complain and cry until finally many of us break down and buy.[22]

Mike Searles, former president of Toys "R" Us lays it out: "All of these people understand something that is very basic and logical, that if you own this child at an early age, you can own this child for years to come. . . . Companies are saying, 'Hey, I want to own the kid younger and younger and younger.'"[23]

When businesses seek to "own the kid" and look for evermore so-

[19]"Watch Out for Children: A Mothers' Statement to Advertisers," The Motherhood Project, Institute for American Values, 2001, accessed August 19, 2009 <www.americanvalues.org/pdfs/watchout.pdf>.
[20]Ibid., p. 12.
[21]Ibid., pp. 12-13.
[22]Ibid., p. 14.
[23]Ibid., p. 12.

phisticated means of targeting the most vulnerable of all human beings with their advertising pitches, they have fallen far away from the Garden's concern for the common good and respect for the dignity of all individuals. The Fall is at work.

*Payment of bribes.* Justice is regularly subverted in business transactions through the payment of bribes. Bribes, of course, come in a variety of flavors. In some instances—for example, the payment of a relatively small and well-established amount to a custom officer for expedited processing—the payment of a bribe provides little or no competitive advantage and might be better characterized as a gift, tip or incidental fee. In other cases, however, a bribe is paid to secure a contract that would otherwise have been awarded to a competitor. In still other cases bribes are paid to subvert justice and avoid prosecution for criminal wrongdoing.

Each payment of a bribe, regardless of how large or small, contributes to a culture of corruption. This, in turn, increases opportunity for organized crime, undermines the legitimacy of government and substantially increases the uncertainty associated with investments, thereby driving up the costs of doing business for everyone in the jurisdiction. Moreover, at least in the case of bribes used to secure a competitive advantage or to subvert justice, under-the-table payments often represent the exercise of power by dominant persons to the disadvantage of the poor and powerless.

> Do not pervert justice or show partiality. Do not accept a bribe, for a bribe blinds the eyes of the wise and twists the words of the righteous. Follow justice and justice alone, so that you may live and possess the land the LORD your God is giving you. (Deuteronomy 16:19-20)

*Growing disparities of income.* According to the Economic Policy Institute, in 1965 the average salary for a U.S. CEO of a major corporation exceeded the average employee's wage by a factor of 24. By 2007 it was up to a factor of 275.[24] It is hard to imagine how such a huge increase in the range of salaries could ever be justified in terms of the relative increase in contribution and indeed, the facts appear to the con-

---

[24]Lawrence Mishel, Jared Bernstein and Heidi Shierholz, *The State of Working America 2008/2009* (Ithaca, N.Y.: ILR Press, 2009), fig. 3AE.

trary. Often CEO's continue to see their income increase even as the overall value of their companies decline. For example, in 2002 the median compensation of CEOs climbed 14 percent. During the same year, the S&P 500 was down 22.1 percent.[25]

The growing spread in salaries reflects not only substantial income growth for senior officers but also stagnant or declining wages at the lower levels of the pay scale. As of the end of 2007, the United States had enjoyed a number of years of solid economic growth. Still, since 1999, the median U.S. household income (adjusted for inflation) had actually slightly declined.[26]

Wide disparities in income threaten Garden shalom in a variety of ways. For one, individuals are psychologically able to relate to those whose circumstances are substantially similar to their own. When we move out of a certain range centered on our own experience, it is increasingly difficult to empathize or experience solidarity with others whose experience is so different. Thus, the growing disparity increases the difficulty in developing mutually supportive relationships.

Moreover, extreme differences in wealth can tend to become self-sustaining. Structural elements in society (such as poor education, inadequate health care and the like) can tend to lock in lower classes and deny the possibility of individual mobility. This, in turn, stokes the fires of resentment. There are elements of this "rich get richer" phenomenon that can only be explained as the exercise of power and privilege by the rich to the competitive detriment of the poor. Again, this is an aspect of the oppressive behavior so widely condemned in Scripture.[27]

---

[25]Jerry Useem, "Have They No Shame?" *Fortune*, April 28, 2003, p. 57. Based on assessment of CEO compensation at one hundred of the largest companies that had filed proxy statements for 2002.

[26]Carmen DeNavis-Walt, Bernadette D. Proctor and Jessica C. Smith, "Income, Poverty, and Health Insurance Coverage in the United States: 2007," U.S. Census Bureau, August 2008, fig. 1 <www.census.gov/prod/2008pubs/p60-235.pdf>.

[27]"Now listen, you rich people, weep and wail because of the misery that is coming upon you. . . . Look! *The wages you failed to pay the workmen who mowed your fields are crying out against you.* The cries of the harvesters have reached the ears of the Lord Almighty. You have lived on earth in luxury and self-indulgence. You have fattened yourselves in the day of slaughter. You have condemned and murdered innocent men, who were not opposing you" (James 5:1, 4-6, emphasis added).

## CONSEQUENCES OF BROKEN HUMAN-CREATION RELATIONS FOR BUSINESS

Adam and Eve's disobedience in the Garden not only disrupted their relationship with God and with each other; it also disturbed the harmony of the entire created order.

> The creation was subjected to frustration, not by its own choice, but by the will of the one who subjected it, in hope that the creation itself will be liberated from its bondage to decay and brought into the glorious freedom of the children of God.
>
> We know that the whole creation has been groaning as in the pains of childbirth right up to the present time. (Romans 8:20-22)

In response to the rebellion of Adam and Eve, the ground was cursed. Where previously the land yielded only good crops, now it brings forth thorns and thistles alongside crops. It "groans" for redemption.

The Genesis creation account confirms several important facets of God's original design for the interrelationship of human beings with the rest of created order: the created order was not given to human beings outright but only in trust. Human beings were to occupy a unique position in the animal kingdom. They alone were given authority to take dominion and charged with responsibility to care for the natural environment. In exercising their role as stewards, however, they were intended to act to preserve the harmony of the whole *for God's sake*. Even in their capacity as trustees, they were never authorized to manage the natural environment for the benefit solely of humankind.

In different ways and different times each of these aspects of God's design has become distorted. Businesses sometimes act as if they own their property outright and owe no one else a duty to preserve and care for the land. Government regulations designed to protect the environment are perceived as unwarranted intrusions on their rights as private landowners. Moreover, even when more enlightened business owners do acknowledge some duty to manage businesses in an environmentally sensitive manner, often the focus is still on managing for what is best for humankind. In other words the "correct" environmental decision is often couched in terms of making the decision that will maximize the benefit of the natural order *for human beings*. If the development of a parcel will provide jobs and low-income housing but will also adversely affect the habitat of an endangered bird, this is a meaningful concern if the bird is an indicator species for an entire ecosystem that has short or long-term benefit *to human beings*. If, on the other hand, preserving the bird's habitat has little or no apparent value to humanity, development seems like the clear, right choice. The notion of preserving the natural order for its own sake (or, more accurately, for God's pleasure) is often not considered.

A significant deterioration in the quality of the overall environment has resulted from these distortions, and this deterioration has been accelerated by the economic notion of externalities. Businesses today operate in a market economy. As such, the costs of production generally affect the price at which their goods can be sold and, correspondingly, the amounts that can be returned to their shareholders. Thus, it is always to the advantage of a business to minimize its costs of production. Of course, there are many ways that this can be accomplished, including socially desirable efficiency-enhancing actions. One less desirable approach, however, is to externalize costs wherever possible. This can often lead to off-loading costs of the production process onto the natural environment.

For example, suppose that a manufacturer generates a certain amount of toxic sludge as a byproduct of its production process. Where it is legally required to do so, the company treats the sludge as a hazardous waste and pays to have it carefully trucked away and deposited in lined waste disposal sites, where it has a minimal chance of escaping and doing damage to the surrounding environment. Since this is an expense that the company has to pay for, the cost of disposing of the waste in this fashion is captured in the cost of goods.

In jurisdictions where it is not legally required to do so, however, the company has a significant financial incentive to simply dump the sludge into a nearby stream. It is not that the dumping of the sludge is without costs. Wildlife may be killed. Conceivably even human beings in the region will suffer adverse health effects. These are real costs, but from the standpoint of the company these costs need not be captured in the price of its goods. The costs are "external." Thus the company can sell its products for cheaper prices and deliver higher rates of return to its shareholders.

The combined effect of these distorted perspectives and economic incentives has been to place serious strains on the natural order. In the last few decades we have experienced nuclear meltdowns, massive oil spills, toxin dumps, acid rain and many other instances of environmental despoliation. In addition, businesses have continued to extract resources at a rate that exceeds the earth's carrying capacity.

> We are cutting trees faster than they can regenerate, overgrazing range lands and converting them into deserts, overpumping aquifers and draining rivers dry. On our cropland, soil erosion exceeds new soil formation, slowly depriving the soil of its inherent fertility. We are taking fish from the ocean faster than they can reproduce. . . .
>
> Demand for water also tripled [over the last half-century] as agricultural, industrial and residential uses climb, outstripping the sustainable supply in many countries. As a result, water tables are falling and wells are going dry. Rivers are also being drained dry, to the detriment of wildlife and ecosystems. Fossil fuel use quadrupled, setting in motion a rise in carbon emissions that is overwhelming nature's capacity to fix carbon dioxide.[28]

A very far cry from the Garden of Eden, indeed.

## CONSEQUENCES OF THE FALL ON THE NATURE OF WORK FOR BUSINESS

Work was part of God's initial design for human beings. It is an aspect of our identity and provides an opportunity for us to participate in God's creative endeavors. Moreover, work has an instrumental feature; it plays a part in fulfilling the creation mandate. Work is an aspect of

---

[28]Lester Brown, *Plan B: Rescuing a Planet Under Stress and a Civilization in Trouble* (New York: W. W. Norton, 2003), pp. 3, 6-7.

keeping and tilling the Garden. It is an aspect of being fruitful and multiplying.

While work was originally intended as a blessing, a number of changes to the way we work resulted from the Fall.

For one, the character of the work has changed.

> Cursed is the ground because of you;
>> through painful toil you will eat of it
>> all the days of your life.
> It will produce thorns and thistles for you,
>> and you will eat the plants of the field.
> By the sweat of your brow
>> you will eat your food
>> until you return to the ground. (Genesis 3:17-19)

Before the Fall work in the Garden was easy. The land generously brought forth its crops. The trees flowered with their fruit. After the Fall, however, painful toil and sweat characterized the work environment. Thorns and thistles grew up alongside the crops.

This mixed—and more difficult—nature of work characterizes all jobs today. Many jobs have creative elements and opportunities to apply our talents to address challenges in a way that is deeply satisfying. At the same time, however, all jobs also have an element of the mundane, the unsatisfying, the frustrating. Work is not bad, but it is neither as uniformly fruitful nor as satisfying as God originally intended it to be.

In part because of this more irksome character of work, our attitudes toward work have changed. God intended it as a gift, but most of us experience it as a disutility. Employees look for opportunities to work as little as possible. The more time off the better. Employers perceive labor as a cost of production. The less labor the less expense. Thus both employers and employees have incentives to minimize work as much as possible, cabined, from the perspective of the employees, by the need to make a living and, from the perspective of the employers, by the need to produce a product.

When a business perceives its labor force as a mere cost of production, it distorts God's original intent. In effect, it denies the humanity of its employees. Henry Ford was once quoted as asking in exasperation, "Why is it I get a whole person, when all I want is a good pair of hands?"[29]

In the same vein, in the late nineteenth century, Frederick Taylor reacted to what he perceived to be the woeful inefficiency of American industry by developing what he would later call "scientific management."[30] Stated simply, he broke down each work task into a series of steps and carefully determined (through scientific measurements) which set of steps would complete the task in the most efficient fashion. These step-by-step best practices were then fed back to the workers, who were trained to follow them exactly. As Lee Hardy describes it in his book *The Fabric of This World*, "management would provide the brains while the workers supplied the brawn."[31] Individual workers were treated, in effect, as interchangeable cogs in a machine, mere automatons. While much of American industry has moved on, elements of this approach still persist—particularly in companies operating in developing countries.

Today, in developed countries, management by objectives has become far more prevalent. Corporate leaders set overall objectives and then invite workers to creatively develop work processes that will achieve these objectives. Transformational leadership goes one step further and seeks to connect the work of employees to goals or aspirations that are bigger than the company itself. For example, Johnson & Johnson invites its employees to see their work as participating in its overall mission to "alleviate pain and suffering."[32] Still, embedded in even these most benign management systems is an implicit understanding that the employee primarily serves an instrumental purpose: "If we can only come up with a management system that will motivate our employees to deliver their best efforts, we can ensure that we will achieve higher levels of profitability." Work designs that see employees

[29]Henry Ford, quoted in Dennis Bakke, *Joy at Work* (Seattle: Pearson Venture Group, 2005), p. 50.
[30]For a detailed discussion of Taylor and his work, see Lee Hardy, *The Fabric of This World* (Grand Rapids: Eerdmans, 1990), pp. 128-40.
[31]Ibid., p. 133.
[32]James C. Collins and Jerry I. Porras, *Built to Last* (New York: HarperBusiness Essentials, 2002), p. 89.

primarily as a means to the end of profit, rather than as an end in and of themselves, continue, albeit at a more sophisticated level, to deny the image of God stamped on each individual.

One last distortion of work should be mentioned. With the confluence of global competition and enhanced technology, work in our culture is increasingly a 24/7 phenomenon. We are wired and connected. We are always on. We are working longer hours at a faster pace. Since the end of World War II the average American has added almost an additional month of work (i.e., 150 to 160 hours) to his or her work year.[33] This is true even though during this same time period, the per-hour productivity of American labor has increased several times over.[34]

Workers are constantly on call. Voice mail, email, instant messaging, pagers, cell phones, wireless PDAs all blur the line between work and home. They insist on greater attention to work and faster response times. Mark Cuban, owner of the Dallas Mavericks, described his earlier business life in these terms: "You try to do as much as you can for as long as you can stay awake," he says. "What price do you have to pay to win? That price is the 'sprint.' You have to build your business faster than anyone else. The 'sprint' doesn't have a finish line. There's never a point where you can say, 'We've made it.'"[35] Today, for many, work exhausts us.

This was never God's intention. In the Garden, work was situated in a rhythm of activity and rest, work and leisure. The sabbath rhythms were built into the fabric of creation; God, as Creator, had rested on the seventh day (Genesis 2:2-3). Post-Fall, these natural rhythms were disrupted, but God's intent did not change. The rhythm of work and rest was now to be protected through the implementation of the sabbath commandment. Literally, the Hebrew verb *šabāt*, means "to cease, desist" or "put to an end."

---

[33]Juliet Schor, *The Overworked American* (New York: Basic Books, 1992), pp. 17-41.

[34]*Economic Report of the President: 2009 Report Spreadsheet Tables* (Washington, D.C.: U.S. Government Printing Office, 2009), table B-49.

[35]Mark Cuban, quoted in Robert Reich, *The Future of Success* (New York: Vintage Books, 2002), p. 123.

Observe the sabbath day by keeping it holy, as the Lord your God has commanded you. Six days you shall labor and do all your work, but the seventh day is a Sabbath to the Lord your God. On it you shall not do any work. (Deuteronomy 5:12-14)

As Rabbi Abraham Heschel wrote, "The Sabbath is a day for the sake of life. Man is not a beast of burden, and the Sabbath is not for the purpose of enhancing the efficiency of his work."[36] On a similar note, religious historian Dorothy Bass wrote, "To keep the Sabbath is to exercise one's freedom, to declare oneself to be neither a tool to be employed . . . nor a beast to be burdened."[37] A sabbath reminds us that we are not the sum of what we produce and that our worth is not found in our instrumental value, as a tool in service of profit, but rather in our innate nature as children of God.

Yet very few lives today can accommodate even one day in seven dedicated to rest, reflection and worship. Job demands, coupled with household chores and projects, have combined to squeeze out sabbath, to disrupt God's intended rhythm of work and rest. After the Fall, work is difficult, often demeaning and out of control.

## TWO RELATED OBSERVATIONS

*First, creation purposes must be combined with ethical limitations.* After the Fall, even activities taken in pursuit of God's purposes will need to be hemmed in by ethical limitations that were previously embedded naturally in the design of the Garden. It is not enough simply to align our businesses' purposes with the Genesis creation story. Without additional limits we will still fall far short of shalom. For example, a business might be able to produce more goods and services that would enable a community to flourish (God's creation purpose for business) if it simply dumped its harmful waste into nearby waterways. It might increase the production of needed goods (God's creation purpose for

---

[36]Abraham Joshua Heschel, *The Sabbath: Its Meaning for Modern Man* (New York: Farrar, Straus & Young, 1951), p. 14.

[37]Dorothy C. Bass, *Receiving the Day: Christian Practices for Opening the Gift of Time* (San Francisco: Jossey-Bass, 2000), p. 48.

business) by oppressing its suppliers. It might create more vocationally rich jobs for its employees (God's creation purpose for business) by disregarding its duty to provide appropriate returns to its shareholders.

Of course, the opposite is also true. Even a highly refined set of ethical limitations will not by themselves correctly orient a business that is pursuing a purpose that points in a different direction from God's design. Put succinctly, neither purpose without limits nor limits without purpose will suffice. We need them both.

Imagine slipping into the back of a courtroom while a trial is in progress. If you had no training in law and no particular context for the pending lawsuit, it would likely prove difficult for you to make sense of the proceedings. But suppose that at a break you had a chance to talk to one of the attorneys involved in the case. And imagine that she explains what the case is about and gives you a quick summary of the position of each of the parties in the litigation. Surely this would help a great deal. Now, as the trial resumes, you could put some of the lawyers' questions in context. You would understand the goal—the purpose—that each of them is pursuing.

Nonetheless, there would still be a great deal about the proceedings that didn't make sense. When the lawyers disagreed, why didn't they simply interrupt and try to speak over one another? (After all, this seems to work on cable news shows.) Why didn't they try to talk one-on-one with individual jurors over the lunch break? Why is it that some of the evidence that seemed as if it would be most important in deciding the issue was never presented to the court? In short, it would seem that these lawyers could have done many things that would have furthered their goal of winning the case but they didn't. In effect, you would understand their purpose, but not the limits they were operating under.

On the other hand, imagine that instead of talking to one of the lawyers and learning what the case is about, you talked to a law student who explained in great detail all about civil procedure and the rules of evidence. Now you would understand why hearsay evidence could not be admitted. You would understand why the lawyers take turns asking the witnesses questions. You would understand the role of the jury. Still, unless you knew what the litigants were trying to achieve—in other words, unless you knew what was at issue in the particular trial—much of the courtroom drama would remain a mystery. Understanding limits without understanding purpose would likewise be insufficient.

Unless the object of the litigation and the rules of law are considered together the proceedings will not make sense and will not be pursued correctly. Similarly, a business that seeks to contribute to the restoration of shalom will need to pay attention both to God's purpose (object) for business and to the limits (rules) that should constrain its activities.

A discussion of appropriate business limits is often pursued under the heading of "business ethics." The Fall disrupted God-human, human-human and human-natural order relationships. Business ethics can be understood, in least in part, as a study of the limits needed to restore or redeem these relationships. And while a full discussion of business ethics is beyond the purview of this book, let me highlight one overarching principle that ought to govern this discussion.

Much of business ethics can be subsumed under the notion of sustainability, at least if that notion is broadly construed. In modern business parlance, references to *sustainability* usually mean "environmental sustainability." That is, a business behaving ethically should not impose costs on the environment that over the long haul would not be sustainable. Sustainability, however, can be understood in a much broader sense as well. As a business pursues its purposes, it must do so in a way that is sustainable across all of the dimensions of its interactions with its stakeholders. It must be sustainable vis-à-vis its shareholders, its employees and its customers. It must treat its vendors and community in a sustainable fashion. And, of course, it must not impose costs on the natural environment that exceed the environment's carrying capacity.

The notion of sustainability was embedded in God's original design. Human beings were called to guard the Garden as well as to enjoy the fruits of the Garden. They were given seed-bearing fruit to eat so that consumption of the individual items of fruit would not, over the long term, detract from the fruit-producing capacity of the Garden. Embedded in the notion of shalom is this notion of harmonious, sustainable interactions.

Thus, a clear understanding of the implications of the Fall means that in addition to continuing to pursue the purposes of business as God intends, managers must do so in a way that does not impose nonsustainable costs on its stakeholders (including the communities in which it is situated and the natural environment). I will have more to say on this later.

***Second, the market will not usher in the kingdom of God.*** Today, almost all businesses operate in a market economy. Failure to recognize and address market forces ultimately causes businesses to fail. Conversely, alignment with market forces can yield substantial financial success.

As we review the litany of adverse consequences stemming from the Fall, it might be tempting, in effect, to blame the market.

- Because we have to compete with businesses operating in low-wage environments, we cannot afford to pay more to our employees.

- Because my competitor does not invest in enhancements to its facilities, I cannot afford to take a number of safety initiatives.

- I *have* to advertise to children. If I don't, my competitor will "own the kids" before I ever get to them.

- We can't hire the kind of CEO we want without agreeing to pay a salary that is hundreds of times more than the amount we pay our average worker.

- I would price our product out of the market if I had to install filters and scrubbers to reduce the air pollution generated by our factory. None of my competitors are doing so.

- I need to keep my work force tethered to our organization on a 24/7 basis. Otherwise our productivity will slip, our return on investment will shrink, and the market will drive down our share price.

These are not trivial observations. The market is a force to be reckoned with. Still, the fact that the market seems at times to be working against shalom-enhancing limitations should remind us that Adam Smith's "invisible hand" is not the hand of God.[38]

One interesting (but merely hypothetical consideration) is whether a market economy would have developed in the Garden of Eden had Adam and Eve never disobeyed God's injunction. This seems doubtful.

It is not that God does not contemplate the exchange of goods and services for mutual benefit. This much does seem to have been built into the fabric of the Garden. From the very beginning God contemplated work by individuals with different abilities who would collaborate and exchange the results of their productivity.

But a market economy assumes more than this. Specifically, it is built on a number of assumptions that seem antithetical to a Garden economy. For example, a market economy assumes scarcity. It is a mechanism for allocating resources when there is not enough to go around for everyone. There is no market in air (at least not yet) because there is no perceived scarcity. Abundance, rather than scarcity, however, seems to have characterized God's original Garden design.

A market economy assumes that individuals will act in their respective self-interests. If everyone behaves this way, the market will allocate scarce resources efficiently. That is, individual consumer preferences will drive production to ensure optimal satisfaction measured on a one-dollar, one-vote basis. Such a self-oriented perspective, however, seems at odds with the more communitarian, common-good orientation of the Garden.

Similarly, participation in a market economy is limited to those who have something to sell that others want to buy. In effect, the market values a participant based on what he or she can deliver. Payment is earned. This is the exact opposite of a grace or gift economy, and God

---

[38]"Every individual . . . generally, indeed, neither intends to promote the public interest, nor knows how much he is promoting it. By preferring the support of domestic to that of foreign industry he intends only his own security; and by directing that industry in such a manner as its produce may be of the greatest value, he intends only his own gain, and he is in this, as in many other cases, led by an invisible hand to promote an end which was no part of his intention" (Adam Smith, *Wealth of Nations* [New York: Modern Library Paperback, 2000], p. 485).

is all about gifts. God's gracious character is revealed first in the Garden but continues to be evidenced throughout the Scriptures. God is in the business of giving people what they don't deserve. Where the market would ignore someone living in abject poverty if he or she were unable to make a product or deliver a service that anyone wanted to buy, God would never do so. The value of each individual in the eyes of God is that that person has been made in God's image. The individual is God's child and an intended recipient of God's good gifts.

Thus, the market system seems to have grown up after the Fall rather than having been inherent in God's original design. As such, it can never lead to salvation. It will not, left to its own devices, usher us back to the goodness of the Garden.

But, in spite of its fallen character, the market is truly astonishing. Consider a simple transaction. We go to the local supermarket and pay three dollars for a gallon of milk. This is such a simple and everyday occurrence that most of us would never stop to think about the web of activities needed to make this possible. A farmer has to milk a cow. Of course, even before the cow can be milked it must be fed and the feed, (or the field for grazing) must be acquired from someone. The milk needs to be processed. Plastic jugs or cardboard cartons need to be constructed and delivered to the milk processing plant. The milk needs to be transported to a central warehouse. It needs to be refrigerated. Those driving delivery trucks need to know how many gallons of milk to take from the warehouse to each retail store. (Too much milk, it will spoil. Not enough milk, the store will lose customers.) Employees need to regularly restock the shelves of the supermarket. Lights need to be kept on. Electricity bills need to be paid, either through online banking or by mail. Cash registers need to have been manufactured and delivered. Point-of-sale devices need to be installed and related computers programmed. Parking lots need to have been paved. Safes are needed to store the cash until it can be delivered to the bank, where it is credited against the supermarket's account. And so on.

All this so we can have milk in our cereal. Literally hundreds of individuals have performed some work or delivered some product in order to facilitate this otherwise very simple transaction. The marvel of the market is that all of these persons performed their services and delivered their products at the right time and in the right amounts without anyone organizing the whole project. Everything comes together without any central planning or coordination. Remarkably, it works without anyone knowing us or our lactose habits. And what's more, it can adapt almost instantly if we (and others like us) were to stop drinking milk.

Frankly, it seems beyond imagination that such an elaborate system developed by chance. Somewhere in here lurks God's providence. It appears that in spite of the Fall, some element of God's beneficent design remains. In theological terms, the market may be an element of God's common grace.

> God does not allow man's disobedience to turn his creation into utter chaos. Instead, he maintains his creation in the face of all the forces of destruction. . . . Some theologians have called the curbing of sin and its effects God's "common grace." Through God's goodness to all men and women, believers and unbelievers alike, God's faithfulness to creation still bears fruit in humankind's personal, societal and cultural lives.[39]

What then should we conclude? Perhaps the best that can be said is that the market system reflects, in part, God's concession to a fallen humanity. It is a system that helps to preserve order through mutual cooperation without central coordination. It is a system that allows for enhanced productivity that in turn can supply the material needs of a hungry world. It was not, however, God's original plan for humanity. It, like all other institutions, is fallen.

Thus, as we seek to develop a theology of business that participates in ushering in the kingdom of God, we will need to develop a more nuanced understanding of the market. We can celebrate the market as one of God's good gifts to a fallen humanity. We can appreciate market forces as potentially valuable tools to provide for God's children. We

---

[39]Albert Wolters, *Creation Regained: Biblical Basics for a Reformational Worldview* (Grand Rapids: Eerdmans, 1985), pp. 49-50.

may end up concluding that a market-economy, particularly when contrasted to a state-directed economy, will do a much better job in contributing to human flourishing. What we cannot do, however, is to equate market forces with God's perfect will. It simply will not suffice for Christians in business who are committed to the kingdom of God to always follow the market.

## 3

# In the End

My wife, Margie, has a habit that annoys me. When she is about halfway through reading a novel, she will jump ahead to the end and read the last few pages before returning to finish the book. When I point out that the author didn't intend for the book to be read in this fashion, Margie responds that she doesn't much care. She enjoys the unfolding story so much more because she is not worried about how it will end. For example, she doesn't have to worry if one of the main characters is going to die when he is found alive on the last page of the book. I point out that this undermines the dramatic tension that the author seeks to create. "Exactly" she responds. "Why would I want to be tense when I am reading for fun? Knowing the ending in advance reduces my anxiety as I read and allows me to more joyfully enter into the story."

While I continue to have my doubts about reordering the average novel, I think Margie is onto something when it comes to reading Scripture. Clearly, in this case the author does intend for us to know how the story ends. In fact, the Bible is full of hints, sketches and glimpses of what our world will be like at the end. God intends for us to read ahead.

There is of course a danger in this. For some, too much of a focus on the future can lead to apathy about the present. It may cause us to be so focused on what God *will do* that we miss out on what God *is doing*. It could also lead some of us to conclude that the only work that counts will be done by God at the end of time, so we are justified in neglecting our work in the present.

But falling into these ways of thinking misses the point entirely. In the end, God's new creation is fully and finally realized. But the real wonder of the story, of the whole grand narrative, is that here and now, this very new creation is already breaking into the world in which we live. As disciples of Jesus we are given the privilege of living signs of the future reality into the present. Right now, we are invited to share in God's shalom-restoring work. In short, we are told the end of the story in advance precisely because it will animate our work in the present. Having a glimpse of what we are aiming for will help us orient our work today. Knowing that God's new creation will have the last word (and in some ways already is having the last word) should fill us with hope and assurance as we engage in the work set before us.

So let's skip ahead.

## GLIMPSES OF THE END

From geometry we know that it takes two points to draw a line. If we want to position ourselves in the middle of God's purposes and activities—to align ourselves with his trajectory—it may be useful to consider not only how the story begins but also how it ends. Where is this grand narrative, this great adventure, going? If human activity is being pushed forward by the creation mandate, in what sense is it also being pulled forward by the hope that is set before us? And what, if anything, does this have to say about the purpose and practice of business?

In wonderful symmetry the final and fully consummated new creation is described in the last two chapters of the Bible, Revelation 21–22, just as the first creation was described in the first two chapters.[1] And just as we noted in our consideration of the Genesis creation account,

---

[1]And just as there were passages other than Genesis 1–2 that also appeared to describe God's original creation, we can find passages in the Scriptures other than those at the end of Revelation that appear to also be describing the end times (see, e.g., Isaiah 65:17-25 and Ezekiel 47:1-12). There are also a number of passages that point to the new creation that is already breaking into our world today (see, e.g., John 3:1-21; 2 Corinthians 5:17-21; Colossians 3:10; 2 Peter 1:3-4). For simplicity, however, I have mostly confined my references to Revelation 21–22.

wading into the Revelation new-creation account also requires a great deal of humility. At most, we are being given mere sketches of the future. There are many questions we would no doubt love to ask, but many of them are just not answered in the biblical account. Moreover, even the glimpses that we are given are cast in highly figurative terms. Revelation is the record of a dreamlike vision given to John, and is written in the genre of Jewish apocalyptic literature with its heavy use of symbols and not-so-easily decoded codes. So we start with the frank acknowledgment that any conclusions we may reach must be held lightly.

With this caveat in mind, however, what then can we say about the end of the story?

## OBSERVATIONS FROM REVELATION

*In the end, God wins.* For those with even passing familiarity with Scripture or Christian doctrine, this may seem so obvious that it does not merit being mentioned. But we must start here. It is, in fact, the central point of Revelation and, in one sense, of the grand narrative as a whole.

Much of Revelation is cast as a battle. God squares off with Satan. The beasts are set in opposition to the Lamb. "Babylon the Great, the Mother of Prostitutes and of the Abominations of the Earth" (Revelation 17:5) is juxtaposed to God's new Jerusalem. The world's population is divided. Some foreheads are marked with the sign of the Beast. Others with God's name. Some—"the cowardly, the unbelieving, the vile, the murderers, the sexually immoral, those who practice magic arts, the idolaters and all liars" (Revelation 21:8)—are destined for judgment in the fiery lake. Others whose names are written in the Lamb's book are destined to reign with God forever.

In this sense Revelation reflects, in apocalyptic terms, the continuation of the conflict that traces back to the serpent's wiles in the Garden. "You will not . . . die," he whispers. "You will be like God" (Genesis 3:4-5). Adam and Eve side with the serpent against God, and ever since the curse has prevailed. Until the end.

In the end the last chapters of Revelation reveal that God will get what God wanted from the beginning. With the arrival of the new heaven and the new earth (Revelation 21:1), the curse has been reversed and God's intended "goodness" has been restored. The sea, which in the Hebrew worldview reflected a dangerous chaos apart from God, is to be gone forever (Revelation 21:1). The intimacy lost in Genesis 3 will be fully restored. Once again, God will dwell with humanity (Revelation 21:3) and, in contrast to the whole of human experience since the Garden, men and women will once again be able to see God's face (Revelation 22:4). Whereas Adam and Eve were driven from the Garden and barred from returning, now the peoples of the world are drawn to the light of New Jerusalem where the gates are always open (Revelation 21:24-26). Death and its attendants—mourning, crying, pain and grief—will be no more (Revelation 21:4). Instead God's people will eat freely from the tree of life (Revelation 22:2). Whereas under the curse human beings were like the grass that springs up new each morning only to dry up and wither away by evening, now they will reign with God "for ever and ever" (Revelation 22:5).

Human history is the battlefield in the war of good and evil, of God and Satan, of God's kingdom and of the kingdom of this earth. At the end of Revelation the battle is over; God wins.

***Revelation completes Genesis.*** At the beginning of Revelation 21, "he who was seated on the throne" says "It is done. I am the Alpha and the Omega, the Beginning and the End" (Rev 21:5-6). This is a great declaration of continuity. The Alpha who began the story is the Omega who ends it. The story that opened in Genesis is the same story that ends in Revelation. The shalom of the Garden is the shalom of the City. It is done.

From the creation account we fashioned a basic purpose statement for the institution of business. We concluded that business is intended to serve the common good by providing goods and services that enable the community to flourish and by providing opportunities for individuals to express aspects of their God-given identities through meaningful and creative work. As we continue to develop a theological foundation for business, however, we must pause at this point to consider whether or not God might have had a change of heart. Somewhere along the line, did God give up on the original Genesis purpose and substitute something else in its stead? If so, we will need to examine the New Testament accounts of God's saving work in Christ (and the "revised end game") to search for God's plan B. Moreover, if God has a new and different purpose, the creation account will cease to be of importance to those of us who live this side of the Fall. The creation mandate will have been for a different people in a different time.

Perhaps the question we are asking would be clearer with an allegory. Imagine that God planned a car trip to Boston and that God's children (and the rest of the created order) were to come along. As they set out from San Francisco, the car had plenty of gas (and lots of gas money to refill the tank along the way). The road was straight and smooth. The sun was shining and all was well.

The children were to do the driving. They would steer, accelerate and brake as they thought appropriate. To help them, though, God warned that they should not exceed the speed limits. In addition, God always sat in the passenger seat and never slept. God was always available to give advice, encouragement and direction. Nobody consulted a map because, when in doubt, they could just ask God.

Unfortunately, one time when they were behind the wheel, God's children went faster than the allowed speed limits and deliberately ignored God's directions. Pursuing what they thought was a shortcut, they turned off the road, knocked over a fruit cart, ran over nails that punctured the tires and got lost in Iowa. The car came to an abrupt stop when it ran into a tree and the children knocked their heads on the dashboard. When they came to, they did not recognize God.

Now, quite obviously, for the trip to continue, some work that was never part of God's original plan will need to be undertaken. The tires will need to be repaired. The fruit cart will need to be set right. A way back to the main road will need to be found. The children will need to be reacquainted with God. Clearly these activities were not part of the original itinerary.

But the question raised here is not whether some additional activities will need to be undertaken as a result of the misadventure, but whether God's ultimate desired destination (Boston) will have changed. After getting the car back on the road, will God announce that the car is no longer going to Boston but is going somewhere else instead—perhaps Miami?

Fortunately for our understanding, Boston remains the destination. Or, stepping out of the allegory, God's initial purpose evidenced at creation remains the ultimate purpose for humankind and the rest of the created order. Revelation is a completion of Genesis, not a substitution. There is no plan B destination.

The word *redeem* derives from Latin roots where *re* means "back" and *emere* means "to take, buy, gain, procure." In effect, to redeem is to take or buy back. It includes the notion of paying a ransom in order to release someone who had been kidnapped and to restore the person to his or her prior freedom. This notion of restoration of what once was is essential to the notion of salvation throughout Scripture. It implies a return to God's original intent rather than a new or different purpose. The prefix *re* (back) shows up in *renewal, regeneration, restoration, recover* and *re-creation*, words commonly associated with salvation. The Greek word that is translated "salvation" in the New Testament speaks of "health." Humanity got sick and Christ, the great healer, restores humanity to full health. In each case the implication is not that God is doing something completely new or different, but rather that God is going back to reinstate the original plan.

> Acknowledging this scriptural emphasis, theologians have sometimes spoken of salvation as re-creation—not to imply that God scratches his earlier creation and in Jesus Christ makes a new one, but rather to suggest that he hangs on to his fallen original creation and *salvages* it. He refuses to abandon the work of his hands—in fact he sacrifices his own Son to save his original project. Humankind, which has botched its original mandate and the whole creation along with it, is given another chance in Christ; we are reinstated as God's managers on earth. The original good creation is to be restored.[2]

---

[2]Albert Wolters, *Creation Regained: Biblical Basics for a Reformational Worldview*, 2nd ed. (Grand Rapids: Eerdmans, 2005), pp. 70-71.

Thus, post-Fall we conclude that God's ultimate "destination" remains unchanged. That is, God continues to desire a flourishing creation abounding in shalom where God's authority as owner and ruler is embraced by all.[3] Of course, this is what the Bible is referring to when it refers to "the kingdom of God." In simplest terms the kingdom of God is where God reigns. It is where God's kingdom holds sway and all of creation is rightly related to God and to each other. Shalom prevails. In fact, we align ourselves with God's ultimate purpose—we commit ourselves to going to Boston—when we pray as Jesus taught his disciples: "Thy kingdom come, thy will be done, on earth as it is in heaven."

For our purposes the promise of the end of Revelation reinforces rather than changes our understanding of the appropriate purpose and goal of business in our world today. Business continues to be called to serve the common good through the products it makes and the jobs it provides.

***The end comes as a city, not a garden.*** John's apocalyptic version of the end is a vision of a garden city, New Jerusalem, not the Garden of Eden. On the one hand, this serves as a useful reminder of what we observed earlier. God never intended for the Garden to be the end. While it was a perfectly resourced starting place, from the outset God intended that men and women would use their God-given creativity and industry to work with the resources in the Garden and to cause them to flourish. Humanity was expected to innovate and to build, and in one sense the city is an expression of this activity.

Among other things this should help us avoid a nostalgic glorification of the past. The calls to "live simply," "buy local" and "return to a barter economy" so in vogue right now may be tainted by some of this nostalgia. In many cases these are heartfelt responses to the undeniable damage that global capitalism and technology has inflicted on human relationships and the environment. Still, New Jerusalem reminds us that God's plan is

---

[3]"Theologian Jürgen Moltmann refers to this biblical view of the end as the 'doctrine of the return to the pristine beginning' through which God will achieve his purpose for creation in 'the new creation of all things' and [in] the universal indwelling of God in that creation" (R. Paul Stevens, *Doing God's Business: Meaning and Motivation for the Marketplace* [Grand Rapids: Eerdmans, 2006], p. 34, citing Moltmann's *The Coming of God: Christian Eschatology*, trans. Margaret Kohl [Minneapolis: Fortress, 1996], p. 57).

not to take us back to a pre-urban, agrarian society. We are not called to find a way back to the Garden. We are called into the complexity, intensity and messiness of the city.[4] And the city is the place of business.

From a different perspective, however, the city is a darker place. As Jacques Ellul details in his groundbreaking work, *The Meaning of the City*, the Bible makes clear that the city has also always represented the place of rebellion by men and women against God. Repeatedly in Scripture the city is the place where humanity seeks to assert its independence. Rather than grounding their identity in God, the city is the place where men and women have sought to establish identities for themselves. "Come, let us build ourselves a city, . . . so that we may make a name for ourselves" (Genesis 11:4). From the very first city built by Cain to Babylon, the Beast of Revelation, the city is where God is rejected. In it humanity replaces God with a security they build for themselves. As Ellul details, the city also becomes the host of violence, "a center from which war is waged."[5]

From this perspective God's decision to spend eternity with men and women *in a city* is a profound act of love. Reminiscent of the cross, God has entered into the very place of humanity's rebellion and adopted it as a means of grace. What was intended by humanity for evil has been miraculously and graciously redeemed for good.

Paradoxically, then, the city is both the place where our deepest calling finds expression and the place where we repeatedly signal our defiance and refusal to serve the one who calls us. Only God's love is sufficient to hold and redeem this tension. Thus, New Jerusalem reminds us that the grand narrative ends just as it began—as a love story set in a very tangible place. The heavenly city is nothing more and nothing less

---

[4]In 2008, for the first time in human history, more than half of the world's population lived in cities "By 2030, the towns and cities of the developing world will make up eighty per cent of urban humanity" ("UNFPA State of the World 2007: Unleashing the Potential of Urban Growth," United Nations Population Fund, 2007, p. 1). On the other hand, as the world migrates to cities, Christians have often lacked a vision for urban engagement. "Most Christians still read the Bible through rural lenses. . . . The church must learn how to go up to the urban powerful and down to the urban powerless with equal integrity" (Ray Bakke, *A Theology as Big as the City* [Downers Grove, Ill.: InterVarsity Press, 1997], p. 14).

[5]Jacques Ellul, *The Meaning of the City* (Grand Rapids: Eerdmans, 1970), p. 13.

than an expression of God's deepest identity, a relational God over-flowing with love.

**The end comes about through a mysterious combination of continuity and radical discontinuity.** The precise mechanisms of the end times have always been the subject of great speculation and debate. For our purposes, however, one interpretive concern is paramount. Specifically, what continuity, if any, is there between the work of Christians in this world and the character and content of New Jerusalem? Does the work we do now in any way contribute to or participate in the creation of the new heavenly city? Put plainly, will our work last, and does it matter?

Broadly speaking, three answers to this question have been advanced. Some argue for agnosticism, some for annihilation and still others for adoption.

*Agnosticism.* As the name suggests, Christians in the agnostic camp argue that we don't know enough to form an opinion on this question. Their uncertainty stems from at least two sources. First, they argue that the biblical record is too unclear. Particularly given the highly symbolic language used to describe the end times, it is better to simply acknowledge that there are questions that God has not chosen to answer at this time. We can hope for a certain state of affairs, but we cannot preach it as God's revealed truth.

Second, end times are uncertain because we cannot predict the future actions of men and women. Unless we are willing to say that God will impinge upon the free will of human beings, we cannot make statements about the long-term future of our work. For example, if God leaves human beings free to make choices that will trigger a nuclear holocaust and destroy the world, then we must admit this possibility. But if we do, how can we speak with any certainty about the products of our work surviving and contributing to God's New Jerusalem? On the other hand, in light of the freedom enjoyed by human beings, it is also possible that we will avoid a nuclear annihilation. In short, so long as God is willing to respect humanity's freedom to choose or refrain from sin, we cannot say anything about the long-term prospects for our work products.

End times agnostics discourage us from grounding our work on a theology of hope. We simply have no right to hope for the lasting value of our efforts. It has not been promised to us. Instead, it would be better to build an ethic of work and business around a theology of calling, obedience and love, and leave hope to the few matters that we know for sure; that is, in the end, however it may happen, God's kingdom will be established, and in the end those who believe in God and accept the lordship of Christ will be saved.

*Annihilation.* Annihilationists emphasize the radical discontinuity between this world and the next. Drawing heavily on 2 Peter, for them, this world will be destroyed and a new world substituted in its place. 2 Peter says:

> The day of the Lord will come like a thief. The heavens will disappear with a roar; the elements will be destroyed by fire, and the earth and everything in it will be laid bare.
>
> Since everything will be destroyed in this way, what kind of people ought you to be? You ought to live holy and godly lives as you look forward to the day of God and speed its coming. That day will bring about the destruction of the heavens by fire, and the elements will melt in the heat. But in keeping with his promise we are looking forward to a new heaven and a new earth, the home of righteousness. (2 Peter 3:10-13)

They point to the reference to the "new" Jerusalem as "coming down out of heaven" (Revelation 21:2). It is a gift of God and solely the work of God. Their argument is buttressed by the relative silence of the New Testament on the meaning of work from an eternal perspective. Theologically, they ask what fallen human beings can hope to contribute to a future city that contains no impurity and is suffused with the glory of God.

For annihilationists it is not that our work has no meaning. Rather, the meaning is conceived of in instrumental rather than intrinsic terms. It can be the setting in which God works on our souls (which do last and go with us into the future). It can be a means of sustaining life long enough to allow others the opportunity to turn to Christ and find the ultimate salvation for their souls. It can even be of value to those who want to enjoy the world while it lasts and who seek to preserve it for as long as possible, all the while anticipating its total destruction in the future. Ultimately, however, to annihilationists our work has no intrinsic theological meaning. In the end, what we make will not last.

*Adoption.* Adopters believe that our work (or at least some of it) will survive in some form and contribute to the kingdom of God. God will "adopt" (and for most adopters, transform and purify) our work for use in the creation of the holy city. For adopters the fiery judgment of the end times is not the fire of annihilation but rather the fire of purification.

> If any man builds on this foundation using gold, silver, costly stones, wood, hay or straw, his work will be shown for what it is, because the Day will bring it to light. It will be revealed with fire, and the fire will test the quality of each man's work. If what he has built survives, he will receive his reward. If it is burned up, he will suffer loss; he himself will be saved, but only as one escaping through the flames. (1 Corinthians 3:12-15)

There are a variety of perspectives within the Adopter camp. At one extreme is a form of triumphalism that is rarely seen these days. In more optimistic times, however, particularly in the nineteenth century before the great World Wars and the genocides of the last century, those that held this view suggested that human beings were transforming the world for good and would through their efforts one day truly build New Jerusalem. It was a progressive theology that found almost complete continuity between the work of this world and the next.

Most modern-day adopters, of which there are many, are far more circumspect about the way that our work will contribute to God's coming kingdom and the extent of its contribution. The most cautious adopters claim only that in some fashion (that is beyond our knowing) and to some extent (also unknown), some of the best of our work will be adopted by God and will have eternal value.[6] Even this far more

---

[6]R. Paul Stevens, a noted theologian and author writing on the meaning and significance of work, once remarked that when he carves a wooden duck that is a particularly "good one," he sometimes muses on the possibility that this duck will follow him into the next world (R. Paul Stevens, remarks made at the "Towards a Theology of Business" faculty seminar, Seattle Pacific University, June 18, 2002). He supplemented these musings in his recent book: "Even some of my own work will last and find its place there in some way beyond my imagination: cedar decks I have made; classes I have taught; a business plan; a couple of books and the sermon or two I have written; a kayak I built for

modest claim, however, imbues work with tremendous intrinsic significance. Work is not just in service of the soul. It and the products that it creates may have lasting value in and of themselves.

When carefully analyzed, the adopters are making two distinct claims. First, they are claiming that the material world of work and things matters to God. This stands in contrast to what may be the implicit view of annihilationists, who assume the continuation of the soul but not of the material world in which the soul is currently found.

The second claim is that the material world not only counts now but also has some (albeit ill-defined) eternal significance. That is, that some part of this material world lasts into eternity.

In support of this latter proposition, the adopters point to a number of Scriptures. Earlier in Revelation the vision seems to make clear that our efforts will follow after us.

> Then I heard a voice from heaven say, "Write: Blessed are the dead who die in the Lord from now on."
> "Yes," says the Spirit, "they will rest from their labor, *for their deeds will follow them.*" (Revelation 14:13, emphasis added)

In Revelation 21–22, while the holy city is coming down out of heaven, it is still named "Jerusalem," as if to highlight some sense of

---

my grandchildren; and my special made-from-scratch pancakes" (Stevens, *Doing God's Business*, p. 10). Dr. Darrell Cosden has also had occasion to reflect on the nature of the work that will last: "Yet rather than limiting our thinking to individual products of work, it may also help us to think about the cumulative nature and impact of our work on this earth and on the whole of humanity. . . . Today we live with the results, good and bad, of what previous generations did through their work. Every product of work, and every way of working, in some way preserves and develops what has come before. Human beings stand on one another's shoulders all the way back to Adam. Rather than thinking individualistically about the salvation of unrelated separate entities, it might help us to see our work inter-dependably as part of the 'fabric of this world' (as Lee Hardy calls it) that God will preserve and transform into the fabric of the new earth. There will be, no doubt, some specific products of our work that through judgment will be transformed and incorporated into the 'new physics' of the new creation. I am quite hoping that Handel's *Messiah* will be regularly in concert in the New Jerusalem" (Darrell Cosden, *The Heavenly Good of Earthly Work* [Peabody, Mass.: Hendrickson, 2006], p. 115). Of course for the purpose of the argument that I am making here, it is not critical to determine exactly how or what will be built into the new creation. We need not decide if we will be sitting on Dr. Stevens's deck, admiring his wooden duck and listening to Handel's *Messiah* in the new creation. For our purposes it is enough to note that some of our work in some fashion may last. This fact alone should be more than enough encouragement for us to pursue our work with eschatological hope and confidence.

connection between the old Jerusalem and the new Jerusalem. Moreover, the new Jerusalem is said to be built on the foundation of the apostles (Revelation 21:14), the earthly church. Its gates are linked to the twelve tribes of Israel (Revelation 21:12), God's people chosen in a historical place and time.

According to the last two chapters of Revelation, eternity plays out on earth. Believers are not taken off to heaven. God comes down from heaven to dwell with humanity on earth. "Kings of the earth" bring their splendor into the city (Revelation 21:24)—suggesting both that there is splendor on earth that has remained through the coming of the new heaven and the new earth, and that it can be brought into and in some fashion augment the city.

Perhaps most persuasively, the adopters make three broader theological arguments. First, they argue that annihilation implies that the material world is either bad or insignificant. Both views are contrary to God the Creator, who called creation "very good." Second, they claim that for God simultaneously to call Christians to work and to render their work of no eternal significance would be cruel and therefore inconsistent with God's loving nature. It would doom Christians in the workplace to the lot of Sisyphus, who, chained to a heavy rock, repeatedly pushes it up the hill only to watch it roll down again.

Finally, the adopters argue from the bodily resurrection of Jesus. As the first fruits of the new creation, Jesus' resurrected body has a material component and bears some continuity with his pre-resurrection body. Jesus' resurrected body will indeed last into all eternity. It would not make sense to affirm that the kingdom of God is breaking into this world (as Jesus claims and as his resurrection enacts) and yet claim that the material aspects of this world are eternally insignificant.[7]

What then should we make of this?

While there are important truths to be found in all three positions, I think that the cautious adopters have the best of the argument.

---

[7]"The Bible offers 10 evidences of why we can expect that some of our work in non-evangelistic activity may last and contribute to the new heaven and the new earth" (see the further discussion in Stevens, *Doing God's Business*, p. 32; see also Cosden, *Heavenly Good of Earthly Work*).

The agnostics usefully remind us how much of the end times remain shrouded in mystery. They correctly suggest that it is easy to go beyond what we can say for certain from Scripture and that we must carefully restrain our doctrinal statements to make sure that we are not in some fashion inadvertently substituting "truth statements" for what are really just conjectures. Still, it seems that more can be said from Scripture than the agnostics allow, and to embrace fully the agnostic position removes hope for the future as any kind of encouragement for present action. It tends to render Christian hope to a pietistic, "it will be nice when it happens," warm feeling.

The primary contribution of the annihilationists is their insistence on the radical discontinuity between this world and the next. Scripture is abundantly clear that the new creation is God's work and annihilationism stands in sharp (and correct) repudiation to the triumphalism that sees human efforts as sufficient to build the kingdom of God. This is important to hold up in that it frees us from the tyranny of assuming that ushering in the kingdom of God is somehow up to us. It allows for a rich understanding of God's sovereignty and grace to undergird all our work. The annihilationists also keep God's future judgment front and center. This helps us avoid a sloppy theology of business that suggests everything we do will be used by God. It reminds us that there is work that cooperates with God's intentions and work that opposes God's plans. And that the latter will be judged.

But the annihilationists go too far. In the final analysis they subordinate the active life of work (which according to them is completely burned up) to the contemplative life of the soul that lasts into eternity. This dualism not only incorrectly treats the whole person that God has created—body, soul and spirit—it also ends up undercutting the motivation for good behavior and lays the groundwork for a dual ethic that accepts sharp business practices alongside pietistic personal disciplines.

The cautious adopters seem to offer the most complete approach. They can affirm the following truths. First, God and God alone will usher in the new kingdom. God will act through the Spirit in human work, and God will act alone and in a manner that is *sui generis* at the end of history. (In this sense the cautious adopters agree with the radical discontinuity that is the focus of the annihilationists.) Second, God will judge and purify our work. Not all work is equal or will equally contribute to God's kingdom plans. Third, in some fashion and to some extent God will adopt and transform our purified work for divine purposes in the new heavens and the new earth. This last truth is shrouded in mystery, and we cannot without wandering into the realm of speculation predict how or what will be preserved. It would seem, though, that these three truths are faithful to Scripture and afford a meaningful basis on which to strengthen a theology of business.

Miroslav Volf notes that "it might seem contradictory both to affirm human contribution to the future new creation and to insist that new creation is a result of God's action alone." But he goes on to explain how these can be understood together.

> Through the Spirit, God is already working in history, using human actions to create provisional states of affairs that anticipate the new creation in a real way. These historical anticipations are, however, as far from the consummation of the new creation as earth is from heaven. The consummation is a work of God alone. But since this solitary divine work does not obliterate but transforms the historical anticipations of the new creation that human beings have participated in, one can say, without being involved in a contradiction, that human work is an aspect of active anticipation of the exclusively divine *transformatio mundi.*[8]

Let me summarize with another allegory. Imagine that God gives us a football on our own goal line and urges us to move the ball down the field into the opposing end zone over the course of our lives. Imagine that our lives consist of running a number of plays. Some of them gain yardage. Some of them lose yardage. At the end of our life God stops by and discovers that over our whole life we have only advanced the ball to our own 20 yard line.

---

[8]Miroslav Volf, *Work in the Spirit: Toward a Theology of Work* (Eugene, Ore.: Wipf & Stock, 2001), p. 100.

God then does two things. First, God wipes out the negative yardage plays. With those plays out of the way we discover that we have actually had thirty positive yards. That is, the ball sits on our own 30 yard line. We are still a long way from the end zone, but at least ten yards better than before.

Then God—in some way that we can't quite imagine, understand or figure out—simply picks up the ball and puts it into the end zone.

Of course as with all allegories, there are a number of deficiencies with this story. For one it assumes that we run plays on our own rather than acknowledging that even as we run for positive yardage during our lives, it is really God at work in us. Second, no story can do justice to the tremendous mystery inherent in God's final work of transformation and consummation. And finally, the story runs the risk of trivializing the incredible call to work for the kingdom of God. A touchdown is a poor stand-in for shalom.

Still, this may be a useful word picture in at least a few respects. It reminds us that God has called us to work actively for the coming kingdom. This call extends to our whole life, including that portion worked out in business. It reminds us that, enabled by the Spirit, we can in fact make a positive difference through our work. It reminds us that in the end some of what we do gets adopted by God—that is, transformed and added in by God—as God ushers in the kingdom. It reminds us that not all that we do contributes to God's work in the world; sometimes our lives run contrary to God's intentions. It reminds us, however, that through judgment and grace, our work is purified and forgiven. Finally, it reminds us that the final victory—the touchdown in this trivial allegory—belongs to God and God alone. It is accomplished in a fashion that is wholly other than anything we have been doing and so wrapped in mystery as to be completely beyond our capacity to conceive or even imagine.

In summary then, as we look to the end of the grand narrative, four observations should further inform our theology of business. We practice business in light of these truths: (1) In the end God prevails; God's kingdom does come on earth as it is in heaven. (2) Revelation completes the story begun in Genesis. There is no plan B. God's intentions for humanity as set forth in the creation mandate remain unchanged. The shalom of the Garden is to be the shalom of New Jerusalem. (3) The picture of shalom at the end is a picture of a city, not a garden. The end is a place that adopts the city-building work of humanity (including much of the work of business) and holds it in God's overflowing love. (4) The coming of the new heaven and the new earth is marked by a mysterious combination of continuity and radical discontinuity between this world and the next. This reminds us that our work matters and that at least some of it, in some fashion, will last in to eternity.

But what does this mean specifically for Christians in business?

## OBSERVATIONS FOR BUSINESS

God's overall intention did not change as a result of the Fall. The car is still going to Boston. God still intends to bring his creation to an abounding goodness lived in right relationship with him.

Similarly, the purpose of business, seen through a Christian frame of reference, remains unchanged. The purpose of business is still to serve. It is to serve the community by providing goods and services that will enable the community to flourish. And it is to serve its employees by providing them with opportunities to express at least a portion of their God-given identity through meaningful and creative work.

But a consideration of the end of the story does add one new feature to our theology: *Christians engage in business with a sense of hope and meaning.*

Just as it does for Margie in reading her novels, knowing the end of the story should allow us to engage in activities along the way with a greater joy and less anxiety. We design our work to serve both by enabling communities to flourish and by providing meaningful jobs for our employees. We do this as we work toward and live into the present signs of the upcoming kingdom. But our work is not fraught with questions as to whether or not it will be successful. While any given initiative or strategy may fail, in the long run we know that God will secure what we are striving for. This gives Christians who run their businesses as tools in God's hands reason to approach each day's endeavors with optimism, hope and conviction.

In addition to giving us hope, knowing the end of the story also assures us that our work has meaning. In a sense, we can find our own work on the last pages of God's great story. As R. Paul Stevens notes, "even business activity may last and find its place, purged of sin, in the new heaven and the new earth."[9] This is not, of course, to suggest that in some triumphal fashion our work actually builds the kingdom of God. Rather God will take our often feeble efforts and in some mysterious way transform them into useful building blocks for the future kingdom. This means, at a minimum, that our daily work has great meaning. The Anglican bishop Lesslie Newbigin put it this way:

> We can commit ourselves without reserve to all the secular work our shared humanity requires of us, knowing that nothing we do in itself is good enough to form part of [New Jerusalem's] building, knowing that everything—from our most secret prayers to our most public political acts—is part of that sin-stained human nature that must go down into the valley of death and judgment, and yet knowing that as we offer it up to the Father in the name of Christ and in the power of the Spirit, it is safe with him and—purged in fire—*it will find its place in the holy city at the end.*[10]

All jobs have a modicum of tedium. Some more. Some less. But even at the most mundane levels Christians can be confident that as they work in service to their community and their employees, their work has both intrinsic and eternal value.[11]

There has been a great deal written recently about the lack of

---

[9]Stevens, *Doing God's Business*, p. 100.

[10]Lesslie Newbigin, *Foolishness to the Greeks: The Gospel and Western Culture* (Grand Rapids: Eerdmans, 1986), p. 136 (emphasis added).

[11]This of course is not intended to justify a ready acceptance of dehumanizing work and work structures or alienated labor. Many job designs need to be changed, and Christians working for shalom should not accept the status quo either at a personal or a systems level if the status quo is out of alignment with the will of God. However, the reality is that as we anticipate the final end of the story we continue to live with work that is at times irksome. Even where we cannot immediately redeem its irksome character, though, we can still understand our work as potentially contributing to God's eternal kingdom.

meaning in the workplace. According to one recent Harris poll, only 20 percent of employees are enthusiastic about their team's or organization's goals and only 20 percent see any link between the work they are doing and these goals. This means that a very small percentage of today's employees see a link between the work they are doing and goals that they are enthusiastic about.[12]

This is not a healthy state of affairs, from God's perspective, nor is it a strategy for business success. Business has the potential to imbue work with a sense of meaning—the Chinese word for business, *sheng yi*, can literally be read "grow meaning"—and Christians in business are uniquely well positioned to do so.[13]

It may be hard to get excited about going to work if we do so ultimately just to maximize the return on shareholders' investments. By contrast, when we as Christians in business orient our work toward serving the community, we have the assurance that we are working for a higher purpose, in fact for the highest purpose. Each day we are fashioning the raw materials that God will massage into building blocks for the coming kingdom. We are participating in returning God's shalom to the world. The end of the story assures us that as we align with God's work we can work with the twin assurances that the shalom we are seeking will be established and that our work matters. And that ought to get us out of bed in the morning.

## A PERSONAL STORY

This understanding of meaning has played a central role in shaping my own career path. Before becoming the dean of a business school, I was a lawyer. I graduated from law school in 1979 and started to look for a job in a corporate law firm. After many interviews with many different firms, I concluded that at least from the vantage point of a newly minted

---

[12]Steven Covey, *The 8th Habit: From Effectiveness to Greatness* (New York: Free Press, 2004), p. 2. According to Covey, "Using what we call the xQ (Execution Quotient) Questionnaire, Harris Interactive, the originators of the Harris Poll, recently polled 23,000 US residents employed full-time within key industries and in key functional areas" (ibid.).

[13]"Sheng Yi—Daily Mandarin Lesson," *About.com*, February 18, 2010 at <http://mandarin .about.com/od/dailymandarin/a/shengyi.htm>. See also Stevens, *Doing God's Business*, p. 25.

member of the bar, all the firms looked the same. All promised great work, demanding (but "reasonable"!) hours, the opportunity to work with very smart and motivated colleagues, reasonable prospects for advancement, and pay commensurate with that of the other best firms in the local market. From my vantage point they were functionally commodities.

This continued to be true until I came across one Seattle-based firm. The recruiters for this firm assured me that they were different and backed this claim up with two particulars. First, they told me that the partners in the firm had chosen to take more of their compensation in the form of free time and less in terms of dollars. They worked less hard than their peers in other firms (and received correspondingly less pay). This approach flowed down to associates who had on average fewer billable hours than their counterparts elsewhere. There were no minimum hourly goals. Hourly production statistics were not circulated. Although the term had not been created at the time, this firm was committed to ensuring that its attorneys maintained an appropriate "work-life balance"—and that was different.

The second particular that stood out to me was the firm's commitment to pro bono work for clients who could not afford its fees. Now all firms claim to support pro bono work. But for most of them what this ends up meaning is that after associates put in 1,800 (or 2,000 or 2,400) minimum billable hours of work for paying clients, if on what is essentially their own free time, they choose to help a poor person, they should feel free to use the firm's letterhead. But this Seattle firm was different. They told me that they viewed pro bono work as the equivalent of work for clients who could pay, and that I could spend as much as a third of my time on pro bono work if I chose to do so. When I explored why they took this position, the firm made clear that from its perspective justice wouldn't be justice if it wasn't accessible to those who could pay for it and to those who couldn't.

This was a firm that I could believe in, a firm that I could give myself to. So I went to work there and stayed with the firm for over twenty years.

During much of the time that I was with the firm, I was in a management role, serving on the firm's executive committee, the firm's compensation committee and as the partner in charge of the firm's largest office. During that time the firm made a number of small, incremental management decisions that cumulatively had the effect of making it into a great firm—just like all the other great firms. These small steps taken over a long period of time (and as a result of decisions in which I was deeply involved) ended up changing the firm in a way that, at least for me, lost the distinctives that had brought me there in the first place.

After twenty years I found myself working harder than ever, and I began to ask myself why I was doing this. For me (and the answers were different for a number of my colleagues) the best I could come up with was so that I could continue to work on the cutting edge of my field (that is, have cool puzzles to play with) and so that I could make more money. And frankly, that wasn't enough. I had lost my capacity to connect what I was spending so much of my time doing with anything that had a bigger meaning for me.

So after twenty years with the firm I left to become the dean of Seattle Pacific's business school. Why? Because I believed that as the dean I might be able to support and influence some of my faculty. And they might be able to direct and inspire some of our students. And some of those students might end up being successful in business. And some of those successful students might end up being convinced that the purpose of business is not just about making money—that business exists to serve the world. And if so, they might choose to profitably deploy their company's assets and competencies to help solve some of the biggest challenges facing our world today.

That possibility excites me. I feel like I have been given the chance to get in on something bigger than myself, bigger than my firm, bigger than my university. And in spite of the fact that I work harder as dean than I ever did as a partner in the law firm, it feels different. I had lost my sense of meaning in my firm, but now my work feels infused with purpose. In fact, it seems aligned with the grandest purpose imaginable—

participating in God's creative and redemptive work in our world—helping God's kingdom to come here "on earth as it is in heaven." I believe what I am doing now really counts, and that at least some of it will last into eternity.[14]

---

[14]I want to emphasize that this is a truly personal example. I certainly do not mean to suggest that a job at a university is inherently more meaningful than a job in a law firm. In fact, quite the contrary. It is also quite irrelevant for the point that I am making here that my university happens to be a not-for-profit institution. It would have been no different if I were at a for-profit institution. One of the central theses of this entire book is that being on the front lines of a for-profit business (or a professional firm) allows us to engage in kingdom work every bit as much as if we were working in the church, on a mission field or in a university. Indeed, at the outset I had just this sense of bigger meaning in my law job. It is just that in this specific instance I had lost sight of any sense of higher purpose in my job as a partner at the firm. I have personally rediscovered that sense of purpose in my current job. I know many Christian lawyers, who, unlike me, continue to see clear connections between the work that they do day-to-day and God's call for justice. They continue to understand their work as having intrinsic value and as serving something bigger, something more than just themselves and more than just their firms. They are in exactly the right place.

# 4

# Putting It Back Together

We have been winding our way through the grand narrative of Scripture. Starting with of the creation account we have looked for God's purpose for humankind and how in particular the practice of business might help achieve this purpose. We then moved on to the Fall to consider the pervasive effects of Adam and Eve's initial act of disobedience. I suggested that their unwillingness to be "less than God" had the effect of disrupting the entire created order. God's shalom was ripped apart. Every relationship—God-human, human-human, human-natural order—was corrupted and the very character of work was changed. Whereas in the Garden everything was perfect, after the Fall things were a mess. And this clearly plays out in business. Finally, we jumped ahead to look at the last movement of the narrative, the consummation and New Jerusalem. We were reminded that God's final intentions for humanity, and by extension God's intentions for persons in business, remained unchanged. Shalom, expressed in a form that somehow adopts human work and creativity, continues to be God's desire, and in the end God's purpose "will be done on earth as it is in heaven."

Analyzing the grand narrative in a series of steps, however, is a bit artificial. If we still lived in the Garden and the Fall had not occurred, then the creation account would be normative for us. Ignoring the effects of the Fall and focusing just on creation, however, would divorce us from reality and make us unreasonably optimistic about the character of our world and what we might expect from our interactions with it. Unfortunately, the Fall has occurred, and we live not only post-creation but post-Fall. But if the Fall were the end of the story, sin and brokenness would be normative for us. Focusing on the Fall as the last word would leave us unduly pessimistic and without hope.

And living as if New Jerusalem had already arrived would likewise be misguided. Such a perspective could easily cause us to slip into either an apathetic laziness or overly aggressive triumphalism. It could quickly lead to our being unwilling to engage with or even acknowledge the brokenness in our world.

The truth of the matter is that neither the creation nor the Fall best accounts for the period in history that we now occupy. Similarly, the new creation, at least in its fully realized state, remains for the future. We are living in a time that is bracketed by these realities but that is primarily informed by what Earl Palmer has referred to as the "decisive center of history"—the life, death and resurrection of Jesus Christ.[1] While we live postcreation, post-Fall and preconsummation, we also live postcross and resurrection.

If human history were laid out on a timeline, one end would be marked by God's work at creation. Moving a bit in from this starting point we would arrive at the Fall. Much further down the timeline is a point in history marked by Jesus life, his death and the empty tomb. Finally, at the other end of the time line we find God's consummation of history, the second coming of Christ. These four points on the line divide it into three segments and we are now living in the third and final of these three segments (see fig. 4.1).

Although we have tried to discuss them as discreet stages, we cannot really understand the implications of creation and Fall for business to-day unless we look back through the lens of Jesus' life, death and resurrection. Similarly, we cannot fully appreciate the hope of the new heaven and the new earth unless we can look forward through the lens of Jesus as the first fruits of the resurrected life. Put differently, Jesus'

---

[1]Earl Palmer, *The Book That James Wrote* (Vancouver, B.C.: Regent College Publishing, 2004), p. 35.

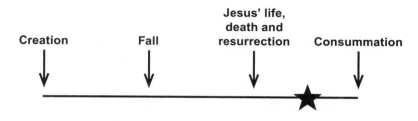

Figure 4.1. Timeline of human history

life, his death on the cross and his resurrection from the dead frame and interpret what has gone before and what lies ahead.

## THE LIFE OF JESUS

Jesus is all about "putting it back together." What was broken in the Fall is now to be repaired, made whole. Whereas Adam and Eve's disobedience damaged every possible relationship—God-human, human-human and human-creation—Christ's obedience redeems and restores these relationships in every possible way.

In some ways the life, death and resurrection of Jesus is best understood as the culminating act of God's ages-long effort to be reconciled with humanity and to return relationships back to the shalom that prevailed in the Garden. These efforts included calling forth a chosen people who were invited to model monotheism and live in a right relationship with Yahweh. They included the giving of the law and repeatedly sending forth prophets. As part of the redemptive efforts, God even allowed Israel to be taken into exile and then rescued. But none of this proved sufficient to undo the curse.

Near the end of his life Jesus told a parable that made clear the redemptive purpose for his ministry (Luke 20:9-16). He described how an owner had planted a vineyard and then leased it to tenants. When the appropriate time came, the owner sent a messenger to collect the rents. But the tenants not only refused to pay, they also beat the messenger and sent him away empty-handed. The owner tried again. And again. In each case the messengers were ignored and treated shamefully. "Then the owner of the vineyard said, 'What shall I do? I will send my son whom I love' " (Luke 20:13). As the writer of the letter to the Hebrews puts it, "In the past God spoke to our forefathers through the prophets at many times and in various ways; but in these last days he has spoken to us by his Son" (Hebrews 1:1-2).

At his birth, Jesus' rescue ministry was confirmed. The angels declared him to be a "Savior" (Luke 2:11). Simeon recognized in baby Jesus the salvation God had prepared for his people (Luke 2:28-32). Likewise Anna acknowledged him as the "redemption of Jerusalem" (Luke 2:38).

Similarly, at the outset of his public ministry, Jesus acknowledged that he was called to a ministry of redemption. Speaking in his home synagogue, Jesus adopted a passage from Isaiah as his personal mission statement:

> The Spirit of the Lord is on me,
>> because he has anointed me
>> to preach good news to the poor.
> He has sent me to proclaim freedom for the prisoners
>> and recovery of sight for the blind,
>> to release the oppressed,
> to proclaim the year of the Lord's favor. (Luke 4:18-19)

Jesus understood that he had been called and clothed with power (anointed) to a ministry of reconciliation and redemption. The poor were to hear again the good news. Prisoners were to be restored to freedom. The sight of the blind was to be restored. Those oppressed in other ways were to have the circumstances of oppression broken so that they too could be restored. And with his arrival, Jesus proclaimed the "year of the Lord's favor"—the year of Jubilee. The poor, the slaves and the landless were to be given a fresh start, a new beginning (see Leviticus 25:8-14).

And throughout his ministry Jesus modeled reconciliation in words and deeds. Repeatedly, the religious leaders of his day wanted to cast Jesus as a judge—as one who would separate the good people from the bad and distance himself from the "sinners." Instead, Jesus repeatedly adopted the role of the physician. "It is not the healthy who need a doctor, but the sick. I have not come to call the righteous, but sinners" (Mark 2:17). He highlighted the importance that God places on the rescue of every individual, describing a shepherd who was willing to leave his flock of ninety-nine to search for the single lamb that had wandered off. "In the same way your Father in heaven is not willing that any of these little ones should be lost" (Matthew 18:14). Jesus contrasted the angry, pharisaical, elder-brother attitudes of his day toward "sinners" with the heart of the waiting father who scanned the horizon eager for an opportunity to restore relations with his son. "But we had to celebrate and be glad, because this brother of yours was dead and is alive; he was lost and is found" (Luke 15:32).

Jesus also joined his teaching with action. Time and again he modeled what it meant to put things back together. He restored sight to the blind (Matthew 9:27-31) and hearing to the deaf (Mark 7:32-37). Many who suffered from physical disabilities were healed just by touching his robe as he walked through the marketplace (Mark 6:56). Lepers were cleansed (Luke 5:12-13), and demons were cast out of the possessed (Matthew 8:28-34). The poor and hungry were fed (John 6:5-13), and the money changers and merchants who were systematically oppressing the poor had their tables overturned and were driven from the temple (Matthew 21:12-13). In short, Jesus understood his ministry: "For the Son of Man came to seek and to save what was lost" (Luke 19:10).

But if Jesus' earthly ministry should be understood as the climax of God's redemptive work, then the cross and resurrection should be understood as the climax of Jesus' earthly ministry.

## THE CROSS AND RESURRECTION

Given that this is the centerpiece of the Christian faith and that it has been the subject of profound and lengthy treatises for nearly two millennia, it should be obvious that anything I say here will necessarily be simplistic and barely scratch the surface. For our purposes, however, it will be enough to make four observations that will inform the rest of our discussion.

*1. At the cross Jesus completed his identification with the human experience.* Orthodox Christian theology affirms that Jesus was both fully God and fully human. His death on the cross was the last act in his complete identification with humanity. He was born as an infant, lived a real, geographically and time-bound life and then died. If Jesus had not died physically—if for instance he had just been teleported off to heaven at the completion of his earthly ministry—he would never have embraced the whole of human experience. Instead he would have experienced our world something like a visitor from outer space might—sharing some common moments with us but, in the end, not ever really being one of us. In his love God chose to become fully human, and this work was completed at the cross.

Business leaders regularly face difficult times and difficult decisions. They lay awake at night worrying about outstanding receivables. They agonize over the need to lay off employees. They are caught off guard by sudden changes in the marketplace that can threaten the viability of their life's work virtually overnight. Business can be a difficult and lonely calling. But one feature of living this side of the cross is the absolute assurance that even in the darkest moments, we are not alone. God is with us. And this God is one who knows fully what it means to be human, and can and does enter into every struggle that we face.[2]

*2. Sins are forgiven and the effects of the curse are reversed at the cross.* Critically for our purposes, the effects of the Fall have been (or are in the process of being) reversed through Christ's death on the cross. He who was without sin did not deserve death. But in his love Jesus agreed to take on our sin and pay the penalty for our sin in his own body. As explained in Romans:

> God presented [Jesus] as a sacrifice of atonement. . . . He did this to demonstrate his justice, because in his forbearance [God] had left the sins committed beforehand unpunished—he did it to demonstrate his

---

[2]"For we do not have a high priest who is unable to sympathize with our weaknesses, but we have one who has been tempted in every way, just as we are—yet was without sin. Let us then approach the throne of grace with confidence, so that we may receive mercy and find grace to help us in our time of need" (Hebrews 4:15-16).

justice at the present time, so as to be just and the one who justifies those who have faith in Jesus. (Romans 3:25-26).

If the penalty for sin has been paid, then the curse imposed as a result of the first sin (the Fall) has been reversed. In this sense, Jesus' death now makes it possible for God's original intent in the Garden to come to completion in New Jerusalem.

If this is so, though, how do we explain our day-to-day experiences? Sin, death and the curse still seem to be very much with us.

The Gospel of John records that as Jesus hung on the cross, he cried out "It is finished" (John 19:30). In Revelation "it is finished" is also the cry that accompanies the arrival of New Jerusalem in the final days (Revelation 21:6 NLT). In effect, we are people who live between these finish lines. Historically, we live in light of the redemption accomplished by Christ on the cross. Looking forward, we live in anticipation of the final consummation—when God's shalom will cover the face of the earth. But we seem to be stuck in the middle. We affirm that Christ was victorious at the cross, and yet the world we live in seems to be full of sin and its consequences. Is it really finished or not?

This question draws us into the already/not yet paradox of Scripture. On the one hand, Scripture clearly affirms that with Christ's death and resurrection we have already become new creatures. In fact, by some accounts all that remains to be done is to recognize the implication of God's radical activity and "put off" the old clothes and "put on" the new (Ephesians 4:22-24). The kingdom of God is at hand. In this understanding, the final consummation is simply the final unveiling of that which has already happened. In the words of Christ on the cross, "It is finished." Really.

Other Scriptures, however, suggest that while Christ's victory at the cross has made the final end of history inevitable, the full effects of the cross are yet to be experienced and must await Christ's triumphant return. It will really only be finally finished with the arrival of New Jerusalem. The finish is certain but not yet fully realized. The final consummation is not merely the unveiling but the completion of God's victorious work.

Alister McGrath suggests that the not-yet aspect of God's kingdom can be compared to the Allies' successful assault of the beaches of Normandy on D-day.[3] As McGrath describes it, the successful landing meant that victory over Germany was assured. From that day on, there was no question about the final outcome of the war. Still, for millions living in occupied France, the notion of "victory" seemed a long way off. For them, liberation came gradually. From the invasion onward, though, the Allies were continuing to advance, continuing to take more and more territory. Perhaps in the same way, the kingdom of God is "unfolding."

Others who tend to focus on the not-yet side of the tension are less sanguine about this gradual unfolding. They too affirm that as of the cross and resurrection, the final victory over sin and its effects is certain but in some sense not yet fully realized. But for them there is little assurance as to the path that life will take between the cross and the final consummation. In the words of the old Drifters' song "Save the Last Dance for Me," the only promise is that the last dance is saved for God. Between now and then we may end up dancing with many partners— with injustice, suffering, disappointment and poverty—but also, if we are fortunate, with joy, celebration and success. There is simply no assurance as to what life will hold for us between now and Christ's return. There is certainly no sense that things are progressively getting better or that God's will is gradually unfolding. In fact, the only assurance is that at the end of the night we will go home with God.

While the D-day and Drifters metaphors differ in some particulars, both begin with the notion that something has happened that makes the final outcome inevitable. And both acknowledge that there is yet more to come.

Of course, the already/not yet kingdom is a paradox. Scripture affirms both of these positions, and yet these are truths that can never be fully and logically reconciled in the human mind. The kingdom of God is both at

---

[3]Alister McGrath, "In the Light of Victory," from *Making Sense of the Cross* (Downers Grove, Ill.: InterVarsity Press, 1992). McGrath was drawing on the work of C. S. Lewis and Anders Nygren. See also Charles Colson and Ellen Santilli Vaughn, *Kingdoms in Conflict* (Grand Rapids: Zondervan, 1989), pp. 84-85.

hand and still coming. God's triumph is both already and not yet.

*3. Jesus was raised from the dead as the first person ever with a resurrected body.* Jesus physically and completely died. And then he physically and completely came to life. He was resurrected bodily. That is, when he left the grave he had a tangible body that bore some continuity in appearance and substance with his pre-death body. But this body was infused with resurrection life—a life unlike his pre-death life, unlike our lives, a life no longer subject to decay and death. "For we know that since Christ was raised from the dead, he cannot die again; death no longer has mastery over him" (Romans 6:9).

Jesus was the first, and so far the only, person to be raised from the dead and walk on this earth with a "new creation" body. But he will not be the last. Jesus' resurrection is said to be the first fruits, but not one of a kind. We are assured that we too will have resurrected bodies that will reign in the end on the new earth. "If we have been united with him like this in his death, we will certainly also be united with him in his resurrection" (Romans 6:5). For us, Jesus' resurrection is both a sign pointing to the future in-breaking of God's kingdom into our world as well as the first piece of tangible evidence of this kingdom as a present reality.

*4. The Holy Spirit was poured out on all who believed.* In the Old Testament the anointing of the Holy Spirit was extended to particular people for special callings. The Spirit of God was said to have come upon Moses, Gideon, Samson, Samuel, Saul, David and a number of others. But the Spirit was not typically shared with the rank and file. Shortly after the death and resurrection of Jesus, however, the Spirit was poured out far more democratically. Jesus told his disciples, "It is for your good that I am going away. Unless I go away, the Counselor will not come to you; but if I go, I will send him to you" (John 16:7). Now all believers receive the Holy Spirit.

In Scripture the Spirit is described as having a number of functions, but two of them are particularly important for our purposes: The Spirit leads to truth; that is, the Spirit assists in discerning God's will and presence in the world ("the Spirit . . . will guide you into all truth"

[John 16:13]), and the Spirit animates life and clothes with power ("but you will receive power when the Holy Spirit comes on you" [Acts 1:8]). Thus one of the consequences of living postresurrection is that we have access to God's Spirit, who assists in discerning what is right and gives the power to put right choices into action.

## THE CALL TO THE WORK OF RECONCILIATION AND REDEMPTION

In chapter three we saw that notwithstanding the Fall, God hasn't changed direction. God's desire for our world and for humanity remains the same. The trajectory established in the Garden was always intended to—and will—find completion in New Jerusalem.

This is not to say, however, that God has no new plans for humanity post-Fall and post-Easter. The ultimate destination of our world remains the same, but the nature of the work that is needed to get it there will now be different. Pre-Fall, humans were called to preserve the good world that God had endowed and to build on it for the common good through meaningful and creative work—what Andy Crouch identifies as the call to "cultivate" and "create."[4] This included commands to be fruitful, to multiply, to subdue and to fill the earth. In this sense all work is forward moving and additive in character.

Post-Fall, however, a new work needs to be added to the mix: the work of reconciliation and redemption. In contrast to the creation mandate, reconciliation is fundamentally restorative in character. In effect it looks backward. It seeks to restore the relationships that were broken in the Fall.

Like Jesus, Christians have been anointed (called and empowered) to redeem. Their work must not only be additive but also restorative. Where there is brokenness, Christians are called to works of healing. Where there is oppression, Christians are called to works of liberation. Where there is disenfranchisement, Christians are called to works of empowerment. And this is true in all dimensions of their lives—including business.

---

[4]Andy Crouch, *Culture Making: Recovering Our Creative Calling* (Downers Grove, Ill.: InterVarsity Press, 2008), pp. 65-77.

## THE CAR TRIP REVISITED

Let me return to our car trip allegory to explain this a bit further. When God first designed the road trip from San Francisco to Boston, the children were invited to drive. To do this they needed to be able to accelerate, brake and steer. They also needed to know how to put gas in the car along the way. Their work required that they care for the condition of the car and that they drive it forward (cultivate and create).

After the accident, however, other tasks will be needed if the car is to get to its intended destination. The damage done when the car went off the road and knocked over the fruit cart will need to be repaired. The car will need to be brought back to an operational condition by changing the tires. Perhaps most importantly, the children will need to be reintroduced to God and to once again learn to trust God to direct them in their journey. While none of these activities were part of the initial mandate given to God's children, they now need to be undertaken if the journey is to continue. Both the repair work and the work of more driving will be needed if the car is to get to Boston.

In theological terms the unfolding of God's kingdom requires a profound reconciliation of all that was broken at the Fall. This reconciliation, however, was not part of the work that humans were initially called to for the simple reason that it didn't make sense to talk of reconciliation in the Garden when there was nothing to reconcile. Nothing was broken. Nothing was lost. Nothing was estranged.

Now, however, Christians are invited to participate not only in the work initially outlined in the Garden but also in God's work of reconciliation. Whereas the creation mandate is a call to participate in forward-moving work, the call to be agents of reconciliation is in a sense a call to reach backward, to repair and restore so the trip once again can go on. And both types of work are critical. That is, the work of reconciliation is not all that needs to be done, but the creation mandate cannot move forward without it.

What then does this mean for Christians in business?

## OBSERVATIONS FOR BUSINESS

*First, business must concern itself with redemptive as well as creative work.* God's overall intention did not change as a result of the Fall. The car is still going to Boston. Similarly, the purpose of business, seen through a Christian frame of reference, remains unchanged. The purpose is still to serve in two key respects: (1) to serve the community by providing goods and services that will enable the community to flourish, and (2) to serve employees by providing them with opportunities to express at least a portion of their God-given identity through meaningful and creative work.

But while the purpose remains unchanged, in many cases specific business activities will be different. Those goods and services that enable a community to flourish will now often take on a redemptive quality. Rather than simply adding to a community's stockpile of available goods, Christians in business will need to look for opportunities where the service or product that they provide may be used to heal or restore. In other words, a business should seek to serve its community by providing not only additive products but also products that reach back and help to redeem broken situations. For example, a business could provide services that would help clean up polluted waterways and toxic dumps. It could provide aesthetically pleasing designs for urban renewal projects. It could produce vaccines for diseases that are decimating communities, make available Internet access to economically oppressed communities or publish books that will increase understanding between communities torn apart by racial hatred, and so on.[5]

In addition, business managers will be called to work to redeem the character of the jobs assigned to company employees. By virtue of the Fall, work is not as God intended it. Often it is toilsome and burdensome. While it is unlikely that the consequences of the Fall can be reversed entirely, Christians in management should seek to re-inject a

---

[5]Consider for example this reflection on the work of General Electric: "As an old-line manufacturer, GE tended to view environmental rules as a cost or burden. Now [CEO Jeffrey] Immelt sees growth opportunities in cleaning up the planet. He wants GE to be known as one of the few companies with the scale and know-how to tackle the world's toughest problems" (Marc Gunther, "Money and Morals at GE," *Fortune*, November 15, 2004, pp. 176-82).

sense of mission, purpose and meaning into work where it has become rote and detached. Rather than emphasizing a top-down standardized approach, wherever possible Christian business managers will seek to empower their workers to engage in creative, life-giving work.

In short, business continues to do what it does best. It creates wealth in service to its community. It provides settings where individuals can enter into meaningful and creative work. But because it does so after the Fall and after Easter, it seeks ways that these business activities might be directed toward participation in God's redemptive plans.

Consider the following example: A CFO for a large telecommunications company is considering two options for expanding the company's mobile phone service. Two groups within the company had prepared business plans and related pro formas for two different alternatives. One plan considered the option of extending service into the greater Atlanta marketplace. Under this plan the company would enter the market as the third provider of mobile telephone services, but because of the large and relatively dense population base, it was projected that the company could make a reasonable rate of return on this investment.

The second plan considered expanding the company's international services to several states in India. If it were to adopt this plan, the company would be the first and only provider in these regions. Its prices could reflect, to some extent, this lack of competition. On the other hand, the pro forma revealed that because of the lack of infrastructure and poorer population base, the cost of providing this service would be disproportionately higher. On balance, while the India option still showed a reasonable rate of return, it was less than the rate of return projected for the Atlanta market.

Providing the mobile phone service could, in both cases, be seen as an act of service to the local communities. In Atlanta, the community would be served by having yet another option for service (and, presumably, by driving down prices in an increasingly competitive marketplace). By contrast, however, the service to residents in outlying states of India would seem to be far greater. Those who currently lacked the capacity to communicate remotely (at least relative to other parts of the world) would now be brought into the world of mobile communications. With the ability to communicate remotely would come the ability to learn of changes in commodity pricing that would allow the now-connected farmers to get better prices for their products. It would also allow for an exchange of best practices and for more up-to-date information regarding weather changes. In short, access to mobile communications in these remote areas of India would likely result in a dramatic improvement in the communities' standards of living. In this case (and assuming, of course, that the difference in the potential returns on investment between the two options was not too great), the CFO attentive to redemptive service opportunities might elect to expand in India and work to improve the business model in this setting.[6]

Consider a second example. The CEO of a major publicly traded corporation surveyed his employees and learned of their general discontent and dissatisfaction with their work. Too many of them felt like cogs in a giant machine. Specialization had become the rule. The workers were being told exactly what was expected of them and then asked to perform exactly in accordance with these instructions. Many in the organization felt boxed in by job descriptions and corporate hierarchies. They had few opportunities to make decisions on their own.

In an effort to address these concerns and to provide these workers with access to more meaningful and creative work, the CEO set about to implement a deliberate program of delegating decisions as far downstream as he could. Most of the company's decisions now were to be made by empowered employees. Administrative staff were empowered to purchase office equipment, schedule business-review sessions, and organize and execute orientation weekends. In the factories, technicians who discovered equipment needing repair were authorized not only to make the repairs but also to schedule a plant outage and to order the necessary replacement parts. Recruiting and

---

[6]Unless otherwise stated, all of the illustrative examples in this book are fictional composites. I have tried to draw on a number of conversations and readings to construct realistic examples, but the examples are not intended to conform (and should not be read as conforming) to any particular factual circumstance.

hiring was a team effort of those employees who would end up being peers of the new hire. A driver on a fuel-handling team was authorized to lead a team in the search for a more modern piece of equipment. The driver was then allowed to negotiate the purchase and arrange six-figure financing with a local bank. Budgets for each plant were set by the plant personnel, subject only to feedback from budget teams in other plants.

As the CEO later described it, "Our goal is to design a workplace where as many individuals as possible have an opportunity to make decisions important to the success of the organization." To implement changes like this required traditional management structures to be dismantled and individual managers to be willing to relinquish significant control. While the CEO insisted that the net impact of this radical delegation on the bottom line was positive, his motivation was clearly redemptive. In effect, he was asking how the workplace could be redesigned to look more like God's plan for work in the Garden.[7]

***Second, the work of Christians in business is to be enabled by the discernment and power of the Holy Spirit.*** Christians seeking to do business right are not alone. Earlier I identified the purposes a business leader should seek to implement and some of the limits not to be transgressed. Figuring out which on-the-ground decisions will best serve the community and how to structure and run a business in a way that is both ethical and profitable is often very difficult. But if business truly

---

[7]For this fictional example I have drawn heavily on the actual experience of Dennis Bakke, CEO of AES. AES is an energy company that, as of the turn of the twenty-first century, had approximately 40,000 employees and numerous plants around the world. Bakke's approach was to push down decision-making authority and job design to the lowest possible level in the company. In fact, as CEO, Bakke tried to limit himself "to one significant decision a year" (Dennis Bakke, *Joy at Work* [Seattle: Pearson Venture Group, 2005], p. 100). Based on his experiences, Bakke concluded that "by far the most important factor [in creating a special, fun workplace] is whether people are able to use their individual talents and skills to do something useful, significant, and worthwhile. When bosses make all the decisions, we are apt to feel frustrated and powerless, like overgrown children being told what to do by our parents" (ibid., p. 73). Dennis Bakke may be one of the more extreme examples of a highly participative leadership style, but he is not alone. Based on interviews with a number of different evangelical CEO's, Laura Nash concludes, "Many of the companies represented in this book were on the cutting edge of participative, open-communication management styles long before the concept had widespread interest" (Laura Nash, *Believers in Business* [Nashville: Thomas Nelson, 1994], p. 141).

is a divine calling, we should be able to turn to the Holy Spirit in making and implementing these decisions.

Often, Christians associate the Holy Spirit only with what are traditionally thought of as "spiritual" activities. The Spirit helps with praying. The Spirit is a good resource for us when we are trying to share our faith or are making difficult life decisions. The Spirit enables our worship and can nudge us to reach out to someone who needs our comfort.

But the central thesis of this book is that businessmen and businesswomen can do kingdom work in their daily, material jobs. If so, we ought to expect to find the Holy Spirit active in business as well. This means that both as individuals and within the context of Christian community, Christians should seek and expect the Spirit's guidance when deciding whether to make an acquisition, whether to hire an intern, whether to set up an online distribution channel, whether to skip a meeting and the like. It means that God's Spirit can be called on to clothe the businessperson with power as he or she calls on a potential new customer, builds a new manufacturing facility, markets a new product line, negotiates a contract or resists the temptation to cut an ethical corner. Of course, the Spirit does not guarantee profitability, enhanced market share or promotions. But the promise of the Holy Spirit does assure us that as we are called to be God's stewards in business we are not called to do it on our own. We are not expected to fulfill the creation and redemption mandates in business relying solely on our own wisdom, judgment and perseverance. The same God who calls us to these high standards provides us with access to the discernment and power that will enable us to fulfill them.

*Third, for now, business operates in the messy middle.* Christians in business should reject the sentiments behind two popular phrases: "Business ethics is an oxymoron" and "Good ethics is good business." The first of these phrases suggests that there is an inevitable conflict between behaving ethically (or, within a Christian context, in accordance with God's direction) and being successful in business. Experience suggests the contrary. There are many acts that are both consistent with God's desires and likely to benefit a business' bottom line. Being sensitive to and respectful of employees is the right thing to do, but it will also tend to reduce turnover, lower costs and increase margins. Being honest and transparent with customers is the right thing to do, but it will also build brand loyalty, increase sales and increase corporate profits. Thus, in many cases Christians should expect to find an alignment between ethical behavior and business success. But not always.

The "good ethics is good business" quote is a favorite among business people seeking to reconcile the demands of their Christian discipleship with their vocation as businesspersons. "At least in the long run," they say, "a good ethical decision will *always* redound to the bottom line." There is, however, simply no reason to believe that this should be true. First, with the increasing volatility of the capital markets, those who do not prosper in the short term often do not survive to the long term. More fundamentally, however, market forces do not always point in the direction of God's kingdom values. At times, Adam Smith's invisible hand and the hand of God may point in opposite directions.

Christians need to recognize that they are operating "between the finish lines." Their businesses function in a messy world. In some senses Christ's victory is assured but not yet fully evident. Specifically, this means that Christians in business need to remain attentive to possible dissonance as they ply their craft. Nurturing a regular and conscious time of interacting with God and regularly bringing business practices into our prayers may be a piece of this enhanced attentiveness. In addition, various traditional spiritual disciplines such as confession, fasting, participating in Christian community life, sabbath-keeping and the like may be useful in cultivating this consciousness.

Simply recognizing potential dissonance, however, is not enough. Christians in business should become experts in looking for the creative "third way"—the way that is not one of the options initially considered, but a way that emerges as the business leader persists in living both as a faithful disciple and as a successful businessperson.

> In many cases, however, [a Christian's] seeking leads to the creation of third alternatives that are more in line with biblical values and that often are strokes of economic brilliance as well. That is why I refer to

[these] tensions as creative tensions. To the seeker, business is not simply a temptation that is to be mitigated by making unprofitable economic decisions or that is to be offset by charitable activities. Rather, his business conduct becomes one more expression of faith.[8]

Indeed, there is reason to suspect that Christians should become some of the most creative innovators in business. As the old maxim suggests, "necessity is the mother of invention." When Christians become aware of tensions between their vocation as followers of Christ and their vocation as businesspersons, they must work harder to uncover new possibilities consistent with both callings.

Consider Edgar's story. Edgar is a vice president in charge of the short-haul trucking division of a large logistics company and has been given sales and margin targets that he is responsible for achieving. In the past Edgar has consistently exceeded his goals—often by wide margins—but this year he is facing a new challenge. Three factors are beginning to choke his profitability. First, fuel prices have risen dramatically. Second, several of his large local customers have sold their companies to national firms who have transferred all of their transportation business to large national trucking companies. And third, the state has passed new emission standards for trucks operating in urban regions of the state that will require Edgar to retrofit his fleet at significant expense sometime in the next three years.

Edgar considers his options. He supervises thirteen nonunion drivers. Most of them have been with the company for a long time and have families that they are supporting. All of them receive wages that are slightly above what their union counterparts are making and well above the market for other nonunion drivers. The wage scale is also well above the legally required minimum wage, but near the level of a "livable wage" in the local region. Unemployment is relatively high, and Edgar always has many applicants to choose from whenever a driving job opens up.

Edgar's company services a number of retail and wholesale operations across a fairly wide region. Most of the pickups and deliveries are

---

[8]Nash, *Believers in Business*, p. 46.

concentrated in two urban regions, but the company also provides services to a handful of outlying locations. Edgar has recognized for some time that service to these outliers is not cost-effective. He also knows that in the current down market a number of these more distant companies might actually go out of business if his trucks ceased to service them.

Finally, Edgar knows that his industry association is actively lobbying the legislature to reverse the enhanced emission standards before they take effect. No one in the industry is doing anything to their trucks pending the outcome of the legislative effort. Moreover, even if the effort to reverse the standards fails, most companies plan to delay the capital outlay needed to upgrade their fleets until the last possible moment.

Edgar is not sure what to do. On the one hand, the choice seems obvious. He can substantially reduce the drivers' wages. Most of them will stay with the company out of loyalty (and because in the down economy there are not many other options for them to pursue). He can cut off service to outlying locations, and he can delay making any expenditures to retrofit his trucks. Following this strategy will likely allow Edgar to meet (and probably exceed) his targets once again.

The problem, however, is that Edgar is committed to trying to live faithfully as Christ's disciple. He is troubled by the consequences that would flow from implementing this strategy. It would result in a number of his workers receiving substantially less than they would need to live on. It would result in significant hardships for some of the outlying businesses, and it would end up further polluting the environment. Of course, Edgar knows that he can't ignore his company's targets and continue with business as usual. Caught in the tension, Edgar searches for a third way. He reads Scriptures. He seeks the counsel of other Christians. He prays.

Here is what Edgar decides to do: First, he goes to his work force and asks for a reduction in wages down to union-wage levels. There is no way that any plan will pencil out unless his wages are cut somewhat and even though this will drop these workers a bit below the livable wage standard, there really is no alternative. Edgar commits to raising the salaries back to their current levels as soon as the market will allow.

Next, Edgar visits each of the outlying companies that his trucks currently service to ascertain which of them are truly dependent on his company and have no reasonable alternatives. For the truly dependent companies, Edgar offers to continue service at essentially subsidized rates. The companies, however, will need to split the amount of the subsidy with him in the form of higher charges. To sweeten this deal, Edgar commits to use the additional amounts collected from these higher rates (along with some of his own funds) to promptly retrofit his trucks. This appeals to the green instincts of some of his customers. It also has the added benefit of allowing some of them to apply for green grants from local governments and organizations to help defray their additional costs.

Finally, Edgar enters into an agreement with one of large national truck companies to serve as their local subcontractor. His trucks will pick up goods at the company's regional transfer station and deliver them to local companies. They will also feed shipments from their local customers back to the national company when long-haul deliveries are needed. This arrangement makes sense to the national truck company for a couple of reasons. They now have a dedicated flow of long-haul jobs from a well-established local company. And they won't need to upgrade their trucks because the local trips into urban areas will be subcontracted to Edgar's green fleet.

By his calculations Edgar believes that these steps (along with a renewed marketing effort focused on being the first environmentally friendly fleet in the area) will likely make it possible for him to meet the targets he has been given. He is unlikely to substantially exceed the targets this time around, but given the other considerations this seems to him like a reasonable tradeoff.

The point of this story is simple. Edgar's commitment to practice business as a disciple of Jesus made him unwilling to accept the simple, straightforward solution. It made him look for another way that would allow his company to continue to support the flourishing of his community, to continue to provide for his employees and to still be reasonably profitable. Being a Christian in business isn't easier. In some ways it's harder. But it is also more richly satisfying as it allows us to align our business activities with God's creative and redemptive work. We have the privilege of living signs of his coming kingdom into this messy world.

## CONCLUSION

The purpose of business is to serve. In particular, it serves by making goods and services available to the community that will enable the community to flourish. And it provides meaningful and creative jobs for its employees. Because of Christ's life, death and resurrection, as we engage in this work we can be led and empowered by the Holy Spirit. Our work can have an additive, creation-mandate feature, but it will also be designed to participate in the restorative, redeeming and reconciling work that was at the heart of Christ's ministry. We do this work today in the messy middle as we wait for, work for and long for the full arrival of "the new heaven and the new earth."

# 5

# Postures of Engagement

## FIRST EXCURSUS

Imagine that you are employed by a large U.S.-based company that sells gold at wholesale to jewelers. You have been offered a promotion to become the senior vice president in charge of production. If you accept the position, you will be stationed overseas and supervise the company's mining operations.

Before accepting the promotion, however, you tour the company's various sites around the world and are shocked by what you see. In several locations the company's mining operations appear, at best, primitive and dehumanizing. In one location you stand at the top of a huge hole of mud. You estimate that the hole is at least two hundred feet deep and, at the top, an acre in size. Hundreds of miners are in the hole. These men are covered from head to toe with black mud, and from a distance, the whole scene looks like an active colony of ants. As you watch, you focus on one man and quickly realize what his day consists of. He is carefully making his way down the steep and slippery sides of the hole on rudimentary paths and foot holes that have been roughly hewn by an earlier traveler. At the bottom, he opens the burlap sack that he has been carrying and using a trowel fills it with wet dirt. He then places the sack on his back (or on his shoulder or head) and carefully navigates his way to the top of the hole. On his way up he makes room for others coming down. At the top of the hole, his bag is weighed and the aggregate poundage tallied opposite his name. The dirt is then emptied into a small machine that will separate the dirt and mud from small flecks and occasional nuggets of gold. He is paid daily based on the amount of dirt he brings up from the bottom. A ten hour day of this grueling work in the hot sun yields a relatively meager payment.

As a committed Christian you are deeply troubled by the degrading and dangerous treatment of these employees. For years now you have been a participant in a weekly Bible study with a small group of friends. These friends know you very well and are themselves deeply committed Christians. You decide to present your decision and your concerns to them for their advice. Each of them responds somewhat differently.

***Will.*** Don't take the job. Things need to change and change doesn't usually happen from the inside. Most of the time change happens from the outside. If you think about how Jesus lived, he never tried to get inside any of the corrupt institutions of his day and reform them from within. Rather, he stood outside of them and spoke the truth. I think as a strategic matter your best hope for changing the circumstances that these mining employees are facing is to publicly turn down the promotion and perhaps even quit the company. The conditions under which your company is making its profits are fundamentally antithetical to the call of God. Your company treats human beings like insects rather than like individuals made in God's image. Sometimes you just have to say no. Besides, I have a deeper objection to your taking this promotion. You seem to be considering it on the assumption that you have some obligation to try to change this situation. I'm not sure that's right. I think your fundamental obligation is to live faithfully for the kingdom of God, anticipating the day when God will come and make everything right. Making things right is God's job, not yours. I would encourage you to find a setting in which you can live more consistently with God's values and look forward to God's coming kingdom.

***Emily.*** Whoa! That is way too pessimistic. You seem to be missing some very important facts here. Consider this. Why are there so many of these mine employees willing to work under these conditions? I'll tell you why. It's because working at this mine is a far better option than the other alternatives available to them. If the mine wasn't there, these folks would probably starve. In other words, this is God's way of providing for them and of allowing them to keep themselves and their families alive. What if everyone were to consider that this type of mining is too sinful and walk away? What would happen to the miners then? Moreover, I suspect that when you get there, you'll discover that there are many principles of justice at work within that particular system. Those employees who work harder and act with integrity are going to get noticed by the management of the operation and will be given opportunities to rise within the organization. In fact, for those employees who exhibit what we've been talking about as kingdom values, this whole operation is likely to be their ticket out of poverty. Now, I'm not saying that there won't be possibilities for improving the working conditions of these employees. I suspect that a lot of the way the mines are managed is simply the result of unenlightened leadership. I suspect you will be able to introduce many reforms that will improve these employees' lot in life and at the same time actually make more money for the company. Go for it.

***Jamal.*** Frankly, I disagree with Will as well. Listen, I know that it is tough. As you describe the situation, it turns my stomach. Still, Jesus calls us to "to be in the world and not of the world." I think that if you turned down the promotion just because you are troubled by the working conditions of the mine employees, you would not be faithful to his call to be "in the world." I think that you should accept the promotion. That can't be the end of it, however. You need to be sure that you don't become "of the world." You need to look for opportunities to shine the light of Christ into this situation. Part of your ministry can be to make sure that the senior management of your company understands the circumstances. You should try to encourage change. Find common cause with the many values that you and others in the company (Christians and non-Christians alike) share. Talk to them about issues of fairness and accountability. Everyone believes in these ideas. While I think Emily may understate some of the differences between your perspectives and those of others in your company, ultimately you may be able to achieve some changes from these commonly shared ideas and use them as a platform to introduce others in your company to some higher-order Christian values. In any event, I think you should go and see what God wants to do through you in this situation.

*Ethan.* Well I also strongly disagree with Will, but for very different reasons. Will is wrong because there is no place that we can live that is free and clear of sin. There's no pure mountaintop that we can retire to and live insulated lives based on kingdom ideals. But Emily and Jamal are wrong too. They seem to be suggesting that your Christian faith will fit neatly with the demands of this job. Let's face it. We have been thrust into an evil world and are required, as best we can, to live faithful lives in this context. The best we can hope for is to be a "dimly burning wick." Everything is just too damp to expect a brighter light than that. I think you should take the promotion because it seems like God has brought this to you, and it makes sense given the trajectory of your life so far. I don't think, however, that you should go with very high hopes of making big changes. I suspect that you'll find that the system in place is there because that's what's needed in order to mine the gold in an economically efficient manner. Consequently, your choice will be to help your company make the return it wants to make or to try to improve the lives of these workers. I don't think you'll be able to have it both ways. The sad reality is that you're going to have to live in a sinful world and, in many ways, even participate in that sin. You don't really have a choice. At the same time, you can be confident that you're living in the kingdom of God. Christ was victorious on the cross and his victory is assured. You just have to live in these two realities side by side. In fact, you will need to confess your sin each evening even as you know that you'll be getting up the next morning to do it again. There is no getting away from the evil we must participate in even as we live in the kingdom of God. Go. Do your best. Confess your sins often and entrust yourself to the grace of God.

*Anna.* I generally agree with Ethan, but I am not nearly as pessimistic as he is about your options. I think both Emily and Jamal don't understand the extent of the conflict that you will be facing, and Ethan is right to call that out. But I think you can be a tremendous force for good. Let me remind you of a couple of things. Will is wrong. Change usually happens from the inside. If you were to close your eyes to this situation, refuse the promotion and even quit the company, you wouldn't be doing anything for those mining employees. We need to be those who bring God's gospel to the world, not just in words that tell of God's love but in lives that model that love. When we put ourselves in diffi-cult situations like the one you are facing, God uses our redeemed lives as a catalyst for change. I can see lots of positive upside to your taking this position. You can gradually introduce reforms that are designed to bring the values of your company into greater alignment with God's kingdom values. I recognize that some of these reforms will have an adverse impact on the company's bottom line, but if you introduce them slowly and carefully enough I suspect that you will not face much op-position. God is in the change business, and this means change not only to the deplorable working conditions of the mine employees but also to the hearts of those that you are working with. I think that you should go, not with a sense of dread but with a sense of real optimism.

Having heard the advice from your friends, what will you do?

## THE NIEBUHR TYPOLOGIES

Your friends' five different responses correspond to five types of Chris-tian cultural engagement first described by H. Richard Niebuhr in his 1951 classic work, *Christ and Culture*.[1] After surveying the attitudes

---

[1]H. Richard Niebuhr, *Christ and Culture* (New York: Harper & Row, 1951). I am fully cogni-zant that my use of the typology from Niebuhr's *Christ and Culture* may be controversial. It is currently quite vogue to critique Niebuhr's approach for a variety of reasons. See, for example, Timothy Phillips and Dennis Okholm, *A Family of Faith: An Introduction to Evangelical Chris-tianity* (Grand Rapids: Baker Academic, 2001), pp. 262-72; Glenn Stassen, D. M. Yeager and John Howard Yoder, *Authentic Transformation: A New Vision of Christ and Culture* (Nashville: Abingdon, 1996); Andy Crouch, *Culture Making: Recovering Our Creative Calling* (Downers Grove, Ill.: InterVarsity Press, 2008), pp. 178-83; Darrell L. Guder, ed., *Missional Church: A Vision for the Sending of the Church in North America* (Grand Rapids: Eerdmans, 1998). Some argue that Niebuhr stacks the deck in his description to the benefit of his obvious favorite, "Christ Transforming Culture." His apparent studied objectivity and neutrality, they argue, was really a ruse that allowed him to advocate for one preferred type above all others. Others

and approaches of various church leaders and authors down through history to what he characterizes as "the enduring problem of the relation between the authorities of Christ and culture," Niebuhr groups these responses into five types: "Christ Against Culture," "Christ of Culture," "Christ Above Culture," "Christ and Culture in Paradox" and "Christ the Transformer of Culture."[2]

---

point out that Niebuhr had a very monolithic understanding of culture that probably didn't work even in the 1950s and certainly cannot be applied to the multicultural pluralism of our global world today. Likewise he has been criticized for his single, culturally bound view of Christ. Still others point out that he saw Christ as a somewhat disembodied moral mediator rather than as a historical person who exhibited specific ethics and practices. As such, the engagement of his Christ with his culture often ended up endorsing the status quo rather than presenting a radical challenge to it. Moreover, some have argued that his typologies were inappropriately applied at least from a historical perspective. Anabaptists, in particular, have objected to the ways in which Niebuhr's typology has been used to cast them into the "Christ Against Culture" type.

As I am using Niebuhr in this book, however, these critiques can safely be ignored. I don't mean to suggest that they are unimportant or incorrect, only that whether or not they are correct does not matter for the limited use that I am making of the typology here. I am using Niebuhr's types only as abstract categories to help organize the different ways that different Christians may encounter and interact with different business cultures. And for this limited purpose, Niebuhr's types are useful.

There is a very real range of ways in which Christians approach business (witness the responses of my imaginary small group) and having types can help us organize and talk meaningfully about these differences. Of course, Niebuhr's types are not the only available ones. Laura Nash sets forth her own set of types: generalists, justifiers and seekers (Laura Nash, *Believers in Business* [Nashville: Thomas Nelson, 1994], p. xii). Alford and Naughton do as well: secularizers, spiritualizers, the natural-law approach, the faith-based approach and the prophetic model of engagement (Helen Alford and Michael Naughton, *Managing as If Faith Mattered: Christian Social Principles in the Modern Organization* [Notre Dame, Ind.: Notre Dame Press, 2001], pp. 10-33). David Miller describes the "Evangelism Type," the "Experience Type," the "Enrichment Type" and the "Everywhere Integrator Type" (David Miller, *God at Work: The History and Promise of the Faith at Work Movement* [New York: Oxford University Press, 2007], pp. 125-42). And Andy Crouch, while critiquing Niebuhr, sets up his own categories: creating culture, condemning culture, critiquing culture, copying culture and consuming culture (Crouch, *Culture Making*, pp. 67-73). Of the available options, however, I have simply found Niebuhr's the most useful (and the one with the most well-established pedigree).

Finally, if all of this leaves you unpersuaded, I might remind you that this is an excursus and that my overall approach in this book does not rise or fall on your acceptance of the arguments I am advancing in this chapter.

[2]In his work Niebuhr is quick to point out that he is identifying merely pristine types and that no person or situation truly fits squarely within any one of them. He also suggests that each of these different approaches has strengths and weaknesses (although, for what is obviously his preferred type, "Christ the Transformer of Culture," he fails to note any particular weaknesses). And of course, as I use this approach, I do so fully conscious of the fact that all typologies are necessarily artificial and static, and do not map exactly to any particular dynamic experience on the ground. I will try, however, to use these types as Niebuhr intended—as useful tools to help

***Christ Against Culture.*** In our hypothetical Bible study, this is Will's position. Get out! The world is a muddy hole of injustice and degradation. Find some clean place to stand and wait. It is not your job to try to fix it. Leave that to God.

Christ Against Culture sets the call of Christ against the call of culture. It represents a form of shouting from the outside. Because of the fallen nature of the world and its institutions Christians are to remove themselves and to decline to participate.[3] As Louke van Wensveen Siker indicates, when applied to business ethics this position is fundamentally antibusiness. Often, in less thoughtful hands, this position finds expression in a naive chastisement of businesspersons. Business is characterized as nothing more than the expression of sinful greed with resulting unjust and destructive consequences. Good Christians don't do business.

There is another prevalent and perhaps even more pernicious view that might also be included under this type. This is exemplified by the famous analogy of business to a poker game. In his well-known *Harvard Business Review* article, Albert Carr suggests that the practice of business can be approached like a game of cards. No one thinks less of a player at the poker table who bluffs successfully. It is all part of the game. If, on the other hand, this same person were to bluff his children, his wife or his fellow parishioners, we would be quick to accuse him of unethical behavior. His conclusion: there are separate ethics for separate spheres of life.

---

organize a wide range of Christian responses to the question of how best to live after Easter and before the consummation.

In an insightful article translating the *Christ and Culture* types into the business realm, Louke van Wensveen Siker links the different Niebuhr types to different approaches to business ethics. She suggests the following parallels: Christ Against Business, Christ of Business, Christ Above Business, Christ and Business in Paradox, and Christ Transforming Business (Louke van Wensveen Siker, "Christ and Business: A Typology for Christian Business Ethics," *Journal of Business Ethics* 8 [1989]: 883-88). In what follows I gratefully draw upon a number of Siker's insights.

[3]Many of the early Christian writers took this approach, emphasizing that to live faithfully as Christians means to live outside of the dominant culture. For example, one of the early church theologians, Tertullian, opposed Christian involvement with the arts, philosophy and literature. At a time when other Christians were beginning to try to draw connections between Greek philosophies and Christian theology, Tertullian responded with his famous quote, "What has Athens to do with Jerusalem?"

"The essential point, I said, is that the ethics of business are game ethics, different from the ethics of religion. . . . No one expects poker to be played on the ethical principles preached in churches."[4]

This is a complete separation. Church on Sunday. Work on Monday. The Christian's involvement with God's redemptive activity is limited to certain ethically compatible spheres of life (e.g., the church, the family, etc.), and the rough and tumble business world is simply to be taken on its own terms.

*Christ of Culture.* On the other hand, and at the other extreme, the Christ of Culture model finds no real tension at all between the call of Christ and the demands of the dominant culture of the day. Because of the complete alignment between the call of Christ and the call of culture, those holding this view see no need for Christians to be involved in the transformation or critique of culture. This is Emily's perspective.

For those in business this translates into a complete alignment between godly behavior and business financial success. When someone in business chooses to behave in accordance with God's kingdom values, not only will this be pleasing to God but, at least in the long term, it will redound to the financial success of the company. Underneath this perspective is often an almost worshipful respect for the capacity of the market system to do good. It aligns completely the forces of the capitalistic market economy with God's values. According to this perspective those in business who live in accordance with kingdom values will find that, in fact, they are working in concert with the world. They will be rewarded in this world and the next.

*Christ Above Culture.* Obviously, Christ Against Culture and Christ of Culture mark two ends of the typological spectrum. The Christ Above Culture type is a close cousin to the Christ of Culture position. It holds, in effect, that the call of Christ is not fundamentally inconsistent with the call of the culture but simply additive. Cultural understandings formed apart from Christ can be affirmed, but by a step-by-step progression can also be brought to a higher level of understanding.

---

[4]Albert Carr, "Is Business Bluffing Ethical?" *Harvard Business Review*, January-February 1968, pp. 144-45.

The culturally determined "good person" is moved (typically through a rational explanation of the higher call of Christ) to a somewhat more enlightened condition. Thus Christians and non-Christians can find much common ground.[5]

This is how Jamal saw the world. Find common cause with those who hold similar values, and where possible help to move the business to an even higher Christian perspective. Many of the secular calls for ethical business behavior are entirely consistent with those that would be raised by Christians. It is just that Christians bring something more to the table.

***Christ and Culture in Paradox.*** The two remaining types are friction types. That is, a Christian living in the world experiences a continual tension between the demands of culture and of Christ. The difference between these two remaining typologies is, fundamentally, that one is pessimistic and the other optimistic. Christ and Culture in Paradox is essentially a dualist position whose adherents see limited hope for true transformation of the world before the end of time. At least between here and the end there is little reason to hope for a greater congruence between the kingdom of God and the world in which we live.

Those holding to this viewpoint acknowledge that they live in two kingdoms, one of which is a corrupted kingdom that must be endured. The other is God's kingdom. By virtue of being born into this world

---

[5]In the early church this view often found expression in the fact that certain Christians were said to have been called to a "higher way of life." For example, by the time of Augustine the church had been flooded with nominal Christians. After Constantine (with only a rare exception) it was not illegal or even countercultural to be a Christian. Indeed, many saw a conversion to Christianity as a useful tool for career advancement. Because of their more nominal commitment to the cause, however, these more recent converts had little stomach for the sacrifices made by Christians of earlier generations. Moreover, there was now little opportunity for truly committed Christians to lay down their lives in martyrdom given the government's benign treatment of the faith. What then was required of Christians? Augustine (along with other early church fathers) solved this problem by the introduction of a distinction between the commandments and the "counsels of perfection." All Christians were to follow the commandments (and to do so was to be obedient, free from sin and in conformity with the will of God.) Certain Christians, however, could push for something more, something higher, that is, perfection. For them the charge was more rigorous. As just one example, Augustine required that all Christians tithe. Those who sought perfection, however, were invited to dispossess themselves of all material goods and enter into a monastic community. There is the good, and then there is the better.

Christians have no option but to participate in both. Indeed, this requires that at times they must participate in evil. Such participation is never excused; it remains sin in need of forgiveness but is nonetheless inevitable. Living constantly in paradox, torn between two worlds, the Christian of this type humbly makes decisions on a case-by-case basis. Here we find our hypothetical Ethan's world of "dimly burning wicks," limited options and daily confessions.

***Christ the Transformer of Culture.*** As Niebuhr points out, Christ the Transformer of Culture is in some ways the "glass half-full" flip side of the Paradox view. In our hypothetical Bible study, Anna is the Transformer. Like those who hold to the Paradox type, the Transformers fully appreciate the corrupt nature of culture. However, while the Paradox types see little hope for change, the transformers believe that by the power of the Holy Spirit, Christians can help to redeem the culture (and for our purposes, the practice of business). Culture (and business) can be brought more and more into alignment with godly values. While perhaps never being able to successfully complete the transformation, those holding to this last viewpoint believe that significant steps in the right direction can be taken.[6]

What shape transformative work is to take—particularly as it relates to business—has led different transformers in different directions. Liberation theologians have drawn on Marxist social analysis and argued for a "profound transformation of the private property system." Conservatives often link the preservation of a market-based economy free from government interference to the advance of God's kingdom values. What links these disparate ends of the political spectrum, however, is their common belief that they are called to align the economy in general and business in particular with God's values. This will require a transformation of the fallen world. But transformation is properly the work of Christians, who are awaiting the second coming of Christ.

---

[6]John Calvin is a leading historical proponent of this viewpoint. Indeed, in general, the transformation emphasis is characteristic of the Reformed faith. It also can be found in the turn of the twentieth century social gospel and the liberation theology that emerged in Latin America in the 1970s.

Five very different ways of reconciling our faith with our business. Five very different ways of proceeding. How will we decide? And perhaps more importantly, what underlying theological assumptions will shape the approach we most naturally gravitate towards?

## GESTURES AND POSTURES

In his book *Culture Making*, Andy Crouch talks about the differences between "gestures" and "postures." As he points out, during the course of a day, a person may need to adopt a wide range of gestures: stretching to reach a book on a top shelf or stooping to pick up mail coming through the mail slot. "All of these gestures can be part of a repertoire of daily living."[7]

One of the key contributions of Niebuhr's approach is its affirmation that at different times and in different ways each of the five types of responses can be an authentic expression of the gospel in culture. In business, each of the different types might be a proper "gesture" for a particular situation. Sometimes it might be best to get out. Sometimes it will be best to embrace a particular practice. Sometimes we should choose to simply endure. Other times we need to seek change. Depending on the situation, Jamal, Anna, Will, Ethan or Emily might have the best answer for the moment.

But what might we say about our more general inclination or default orientation—that is, what Crouch would call our "posture"? As he describes it, a posture is a "learned but unconscious default position, our natural stance. It is the position our body assumes when we aren't paying attention, the basic attitude we carry through life."[8] For example, Crouch describes that as an "awkward gangly teenager" he had an unconscious inclination to slump to minimize his height. As a teenager, the slump was his posture.

Assuming that the advice given by each of the members of our hypothetical Bible study might be an appropriate gesture from time to time, can we make any judgments as to which of these approaches

---

[7]Crouch, *Culture Making*, p. 90.
[8]Ibid., p. 74.

might be the best posture over time for a Christian to bring to business? And as a preliminary matter, what might we be able to surmise as to the likely connections between different postures (i.e., attitudes toward business) and differing theological convictions?

## CORRELATION OF BUSINESS POSTURES
## WITH THEOLOGICAL BELIEFS

In short, it seems likely that the business posture that we most closely identify with will be correlated with the answers to three theological questions.

First, there is the question of the nature and extent of common grace. As I discussed in the chapter on the Fall, as a result of humanity's sinful choices, all relationships (God-human, human-human, human-creation and human-work) have been disrupted. None of them is as God intends. On this point there is no disagreement.

The extent of the disruption, however, is a subject of ongoing theological debate. Some argue that God's plan was severely distorted and that human beings are nearly incapable of discerning God's true design in the created order (at least apart from Scripture and the work of the Spirit). For others, however, the Fall produced a somewhat less radical result. To this group God's creation has been damaged, but much of God's original design remains apparent both within and around us and can be discovered through a reflective use of our rational faculties. For those in this group, God's shalom as initially established in the Garden was not essentially effaced by the Fall but rather "merely" marred. Put simply, to what extent did the good of creation lose its goodness and become truly bad?

Second, what will happen at the end of human history? There are a variety of viewpoints about this: some are agnostics, some are annihilationists and some are adopters. Will this world be burned up and something totally new substituted in its place? Will the best of this world be purified but in some mysterious way remain? Or do we just not know? While I have suggested that the cautious adopters seem to have the best of this argument, where one lands on this question may significantly affect the choice of a preferred Niebuhrian type.

Third, where do we place our emphasis in the already/not yet paradox? Do we tend to emphasize that the kingdom of God is at hand? Or do we tend to emphasize that it is yet to come? And if we emphasize that it is yet to be fulfilled, do we find that it is gradually unfolding (the D-day analogy) or that it will only be revealed at the culmination of God's plan (the Drifters analogy)?

Answers to these three questions—What happened at the Fall? What will the end be like? and Is the kingdom already, not yet or both?—can help predict which of the Niebuhrian postures we are most likely to embrace.

For example, those who adopt the Christ Against Culture approach might typically be expected to reflect an extreme view of the Fall. That which was good has become irretrievably bad. Likewise they will often reflect an annihilationist's understanding of the end times, emphasizing the radical discontinuity between the new earth and the world we live in today.

By contrast, those who fall into the Christ of Culture type typically evince some combination of the following viewpoints. They tend to minimize the extent to which the Fall has distorted God's original intent for humankind and the rest of creation. Their understanding of the end times tends to be a triumphal adoption of human activity. Minimal discontinuity, if any, is anticipated between now and then. Finally, they are likely to subscribe heavily to the "already" side of the already/not yet paradox. Truly the world was realigned by Christ's death and resurrection on the cross.

Those holding to the Christ Above Culture viewpoint will tend to minimize the adverse consequences of the Fall and reject the need for a radical transformation at the end of time. In contrast to the Christ of Culture believers, however, those holding to this view are likely to have a more balanced sense of the already/not yet paradox. Christ's battle has already been won, but there remains a need to bring into effect the consequences of his victory.

Christ and Culture in Paradox adherents fully appreciate the extent of evil present in the world as a result of the Fall. They live at the very heart of the already/not yet paradox. They see, however, little hope that our work in this world will serve as building blocks in the hands of God when he rolls out his final kingdom. Consequently, those who hold to this viewpoint may tend to emphasize and look forward to the day when this earth will pass away and something completely new and different will be substituted in its stead.

Finally, Christ Transforming Culture believers, while acknowledging the consequences of the Fall, refuse to believe that the image of God has been completely erased or so permanently marred that it is beyond redemption. They are comfortable with the already/not yet paradox, believing, on the one hand, that the outcome of their work is assured and, on the other hand, that there is work yet to be done. Finally, the transformers would likely reject any theology that suggests that all their work will be wiped out in a final fire of judgment. For them, transformation work, as enabled by the Spirit of God, is actual participation in the building of the new kingdom.

These five perspectives are summarized in figure 5.1.

|  | What happened at the Fall? | Already/not yet tension | What happens at the end of time? |
|---|---|---|---|
| Christ Against Business | Image of God nearly erased | Not-yet emphasis | Radical discontinuity—all works burn up |
| Christ of Business | Image of God only slightly distorted | Already emphasis | No radical discontinuity—works building future kingdom |
| Christ Above Business | Image of God only slightly distorted | In balance | No radical discontinuity—works building future kingdom |
| Christ and Business in Paradox | Image of God seriously marred | In balance/"Save the Last Dance" model | Radical discontinuity—all works burn up |
| Christ the Transformer of Business | Image of God seriously marred | In balance/D-day model | No radical discontinuity—works building future kingdom |

**Figure 5.1. Five business postures**

To suggest, however, that there is a correlation between theological beliefs and attitudes toward business is not the same thing as saying that our theological beliefs cause us to adopt one posture or another. Correlation is not causation, and it is quite possible that the causation runs the other way. It would be a happy fact if Christians first carefully thought out their theological positions and then married these convictions to congruent approaches to business and other aspects of life. In many cases, however, quite the opposite may be true. For many business leaders, their philosophy and approach to business may be much more thought out than their theology. Where they land on theological questions may be heavily influenced by the posture that they have adopted to their work in business, which, after all, occupies the great majority of their waking hours. In any case, in the lives of thoughtful Christians, these two belief systems (i.e., postures toward business and theological convictions) will probably continue to interact with each other in an iterative fashion. Therefore, I suspect that those seeking to live out integrated and congruent lives will, over time, gravitate toward one of the correlations that I have identified in figure 5.1.

What then can we conclude is the posture that God would desire for Christians in business? In light of the theological conclusions that I have previously identified, which of these Niehburian types would it be appropriate to adopt *as a posture?*

First, it appears that both of the polar positions should be rejected. In my view, neither Christ of Culture nor Christ Against Culture is adequately nuanced to describe Christ's redemptive work and his call to his church.

Christ commands that we emulate his life by taking up our cross and following him. We must recognize, however, that the cross points to the inevitable conflict between the kingdom of God and the kingdom of this world. We acknowledge that Christ lived a life in perfect obedience to the Father. The result of his perfect obedience, however, was not material success but rather a sentence of death by the cruelest instrument of torture then known to the Roman Empire. Repeatedly Scripture assures us that we should expect nothing better. "Remember the words I spoke to you: 'No servant is greater than his master. If they persecuted me, they will persecute you also'" (John 15:20).

The cross embodies the fundamental and fierce tension between the ways of God and the ways of this world. Thus, in the context of business, we must reject the Christ of Culture conclusion that all godly behavior in business will yield an enhanced bottom line. Businesses operating in accordance with God's kingdom values should expect that they will, at least from time to time, be required to "take up the cross."[9]

The cross and resurrection are, however, clearly more than mere ethical models. They stand at the decisive center of human history and mark Christ's victory over death and sin. They also triggered the outpouring of the Holy Spirit. As such, they represent not only a call to self-sacrifice but also an assurance of power that enables Christians to begin to live out God's kingdom values in the midst of a fallen world. By the power of the Holy Spirit, we are both called and enabled to bring evidence of God's triumph into the world. "You will receive power when the Holy Spirit comes on you; and you will be my witnesses in Jerusalem, and in all Judea and Samaria, and to the ends of the earth" (Acts 1:8). We testify to God's victory not only in words but by deeds that evidence the in-breaking of God's justice and righteousness ("for the kingdom of God is not a matter of talk but of power" [1 Corinthians 4:20]). Thus we must also reject the extreme position of Christ Against Culture. As individuals, we are set free not only for salvation but also, empowered by the Spirit, to live into this world signs of God's realigned kingdom.[10]

What can we say about the other three positions, positions that Niebuhr refers to as "The Church of the Center"? There is at least some truth in all of these other postures. Again, considering these issues in

---

[9]For example, a business might seek to open operations in a country characterized by pervasive government corruption. By refusing to pay bribes, the business could be forced to shut down.

[10]On the other hand, if a business opening up operations in a country characterized by extensive corruption refuses to pay bribes, it might survive and could have the effect, over time, of changing the expectations of business and government leaders. A consistent voice for integrity and transparency, coupled with a genuine concern for the well-being of the significantly underpaid government officials, might, in a Spirit-empowered way, truly move the community closer to God's intended kingdom.

the field of business we often find a relatively close alignment between acts of righteousness and business decisions that prove financially successful. While I emphatically deny that good ethics *always* translates into a profitable business, empirical evidence suggests that it often does so. In most cases, being honest with customers, caring for employees, honoring promises and the like tend both to further the kingdom of God and to enhance profits. This alignment suggests (as the adherents to the Christ Above Business would argue) that much of the image of God remains embedded in us and in our world, notwithstanding the Fall. Christians can build on and need not necessarily tear down the natural order of things.

Other experiences, however, are more consistent with the Christ and Business in Paradox position. At times, as citizens of two worlds, it does appear that the only choice we are left with is the lesser of two evils. The power of the market set in the context of a fallen world may sometimes require that Christian managers not fully pursue God's redemptive agenda in order to stay in the game. As such, there is no pure system available for Christians to implement. Business decisions require a step-by-step walk through a muddy field trusting that at the end of the day God's grace will wipe away the dirt.

Finally, our experience also testifies to the possibilities of transformation. We are not stuck with the pessimism of the Paradox type. There are countless examples of individuals committed to Christ who have had a salutary influence in redirecting and even transforming the ethics and culture of various corporate entities. Numerous existing businesses attest to the transforming power unleashed by the Spirit through Christians in business.

As part of God's redemptive activities, Christians are called to engage their world. They don't retreat. They don't assume that everything is fine how it is. Rather, they become God's agents on the ground. The three perspectives of Niebuhr's "Church of the Center" should frame their posture. At times, Christians are to build on the common ground that they find between the mandates of culture and God's kingdom. At other times, they will be caught in the tensions between what is and what should be, and these tensions will drive them to confession and to God's grace. In all cases, however, Christians are called to seek out opportunities to work for the transformation—the redemption and reconciliation—of the fallen world in which God has placed them.

# 6

# A Thought About Institutions

## SECOND EXCURSUS

At a recent commencement exercise, a graduating senior came to the podium to speak on behalf of her class. During the preceding year she had chaired the senior gift committee and she now rose to announce the gift. She began her brief remarks by sharing that as the committee had discussed the matter, it had concluded that it simply couldn't bear the idea of purchasing yet another plaque or bench or artifact for the campus. Rather, she said, the committee had decided to give the funds donated by seniors to a local nonprofit organization that would use them to help Central American farmers purchase farmland. Upon hearing this announcement, the students and faculty cheered heartily. What a great expression of the university's mission of cultural engagement for positive change in the world!

The next day, however, the president of the university found himself wondering about this decision from a different perspective:

> When you have a wonderfully talented student stand in front of our students and faculty and announce that the students are giving their class gift to this local nonprofit—instead of to the institution that gave them a vision that this nonprofit was worthy of their attention—well, we indeed have an eroding of institutional thinking, institutional loyalty, a sense that institutions are worthy of our support (we are all about

benches and plaques, the nonprofit is about serving the poor). We've got to communicate a genuine respect for our institution—this place, these people, this hundred year old tradition, these buildings, and the world change we are teaching—or we are dead in the water. . . . There are huge implications for us as a university, or for the church, or any other institution.[1]

At the outset of this book I raised the question as to whether God has purposes for institutions or only for individuals who, in turn, sometimes pursue these purposes through institutions. That is, from God's perspective are institutions of any import?

As our recent commencement exercise might suggest, from our individualistic, Western worldview many would be inclined to answer this question in the negative. As a culture we often exhibit a deep suspicion of institutions. For example, in spite of the many ways that it undergirds our sense of security and order, rarely is government spoken of in a positive light. The institutional aspects of universities are often demeaned. "Real learning takes place in encounters outside of classrooms." When considering which charities to support, we often value those organizations that spend the smallest percentage of contributed dollars on support of the institution itself—as if institutional support is bad or at least a subordinate good. And how often have we heard words to the effect of "I am a Christian, but I have no use for the church"?

## CREATION

But what if God created institutions and called them good?

On nine separate occasions in the epistles Paul refers to something he calls "powers" (sometimes alone and sometimes in connection with seemingly related notions of "principalities," "thrones" and "dominions"). Until mid-way through the last century these phrases were widely viewed as references to angels and demons, and given very little attention. After World War I and especially in the context of the rise of Nazism, however, these passages began to receive greater scrutiny and

---

[1]Dr. Philip Eaton, email to faculty at Seattle Pacific University, June 13, 2009.

new scholarly attention. A number of scholars have now begun to associate these concepts with structures, worldviews, institutions and other orders that give shape to the world we live in, or, alternatively, to spiritual forces that inhabit and animate these structures and orders. And if this interpretation is correct, then corporations, global capitalism, free-market economic systems and even the institution of business itself may be understood as constituting (or at least as being animated by) some of these biblical "powers."

If so, Paul's letter to the Colossians reminds us that in God's original design, the powers were intended for good.

> For by him all things were created: things in heaven and on earth, visible and invisible, whether thrones or powers or rulers or authorities; all things were created by him and for him. He is before all things, and in him all things hold together. (Colossians 1:16-17)

This is a useful starting place because most of what Scripture has to say about these powers is overwhelmingly negative. Still, as John Howard Yoder notes:

> It is important therefore to begin with the reminder that they were part of the good creation of God. Society and history, even nature, would be impossible without regularity, system, order—and God has provided for this need. The universe is not sustained arbitrarily, immediately, and erratically by an unbroken succession of new divine interventions. It was made in an ordered form and "it was good." The creative power worked in a mediated form, by means of the Powers that regularized all visible reality.[2]

A primeval conception of chaos often found expression in the image of "the waters of the sea." This is why in Genesis 1 God is described as separating the waters to create a space in its midst where creation could thrive (Genesis 1:6-7). One way to think of the powers, in the context of this imagery, is that they are the structures—the dikes—that were

---

[2]John Howard Yoder, *The Politics of Jesus* (Grand Rapids: Eerdmans, 1994), p. 141. Augustine said, "The peace of the celestial city is the perfectly ordered and harmonious enjoyment of God and of one another in God. The peace of all things is the tranquility of order (*The City of God*, trans. Marcus Dods [New York: Modern Library Paperback Edition, 2000], p. 690).

created by God to hold the sea of chaos in check. They were originally designed to provide the order that creates the space needed to allow for the nurture and flourishing of humanity.

## FALL

As part of the original good creation the powers were created subservient. That is, they were intended to exist, like humans, to further God's purpose and to bring God glory. Like everything else, however, they were also subject to the Fall. Just like human beings, the powers were not content with their subordinate role. Rather than serving as subordinate creations, each sought to be an absolute authority, claiming for itself the power and glory of God.

Yoder notes:

> These powers have rebelled and are fallen. They did not accept the modesty that would have permitted them to remain conformed to the creative purpose, but rather they claimed for themselves an absolute value. They thereby enslaved humanity and our history. . . . To what are we subject? Precisely to those values and structures which are necessary to life and society, but which have claimed the status of idols and have succeeded in making us serve them as if they were of absolute value.[3]

One of the manifestations of this servitude in business may be the frequent idolatry by Christians of market forces. Many seem to give unquestioned assent to the notion that if the market requires it, it must be so. In giving glory to the market others often attribute certain virtues to market economics where such linkages are not obvious and may not be demonstrable.[4] Still others assign ultimate value to the survival of the business (e.g., "the company's first and overriding purpose is to survive"). Not infrequently, this idolatry is hidden in a dualism that

---

[3]Ibid., p. 142.

[4]"More subtly, free-market visionaries attribute ethical virtues to the market that it does not, in fact, possess. The virtues they emphasize—individualism, freedom, democracy, choice, flexibility, creativity, openness, adaptability, self-improvement, self discipline, leadership, and responsibility—are in fact not inherent in the operations of market economies" (Daniel Yankelovich, *Profit with Honor: The New Stage of Market Capitalism* [New Haven, Conn.: Yale University Press, 2006], pp. 74-75).

gives full weight to biblical principles until they impinge on business practices—at which point they are often regarded as not practical, not applicable or not possible to implement given the competing and overarching requirements of the business.[5]

Another consequence of the fall of the powers is the distortion of the relationships between institutions. As an obvious and natural result of each power claiming for itself absolute authority, these intended allies have now become adversaries. As God originally intended them, the different institutions were to work together, collaboratively serving God by preserving order. When each power became its own god, however, all other powers became rivals.

Traditionally, many in business have viewed other institutions as adversaries. "Government regulation is a burden on business." "Nongovernmental organizations introduce inefficiencies by making shrill demands that unfairly threaten companies' reputations in the media." "Faith-based perspectives have no place in the office; spirituality is a private matter and should be checked at the door." Even families, with their competing demands for loyalty and time, are sometimes viewed as obstacles to maximizing productivity.

Conversely, other institutions often view business as a dangerous force that must be carefully controlled, and sadly the church is often one of the worst offenders. Although perhaps less frequently than in the past, in subtle and often implicit ways, business is still regularly scolded from the pulpit. "Business is grounded in greed." "Capitalism is the source of much evil in the world." "People going into business are just interested in themselves. Working in the 'helping professions' is more Christian."

Church leaders often find themselves uncomfortable with business

---

[5]One of the central findings that emerges from Laura Nash's interviews is that evangelical business leaders tend to think of their responsibilities as Christians and ethical leaders in narrow terms; they tend to focus on interpersonal dynamics rather than on systemic factors of business and the marketplace. When confronted with apparent tensions between business in a free-market system and Christian doctrine, "many of them sidestepped the issue" (Laura Nash, *Believers in Business* [Nashville: Thomas Nelson, 1994], p. 38). Consequently, it may not be surprising that many market believers fail to recognize the potential for idolatry.

leaders, and this discomfort produces a sense among many in business that they are somehow second-class Christians. They are valued because of what their tithes may pay for, but what they actually do to raise this money is suspect, a little sordid and, in general, a bit of an embarrassment.

As rivals each power often seeks to expand its sphere of authority and to protect against incursions into its sphere by others. Business is regularly guilty of invading the spheres of others. By demanding that its executives spend more time on the job, for example, business may be invading the family sphere. By using its considerable financial resources to lobby for special government privileges, business may be invading the government sphere. When business executives suggest that churches and educational institutions should adopt market-based models to "become more efficient," this too may be an inappropriate extension of business authority.

Business also fiercely resists efforts by other spheres to invade what it believes is the rightful province of its own authority. This accounts, for example, for a great deal of the hostility many business leaders exhibit toward any form of government regulation. Laws and regulations are said to impede the efficiency of the market. They get in the way of business.

This idolatry, disrespect and outright rivalry all flow directly from the rebellion of the powers. In the words of the serpent, they too have sought "to be like God."

## REDEMPTION

Just as the effect of sin on human beings and communities has been reversed and redeemed by the cross and resurrection of Jesus Christ, so too the fallen character of the powers. "And having disarmed the powers and authorities, he made a public spectacle of them, triumphing over by the cross" (Colossians 2:15).

At the cross, Jesus reveals (makes a public spectacle of) the real character of the powers. Whereas they have been assumed by many to be the basic building blocks of society and unquestioned in their authority, the cross reveals them as false gods. By unmasking them Christ occasions their defeat (triumphing over them). In other words, simply by revealing that they are not absolute and ultimate powers unto themselves, the cross takes away the authority of (disarms) these institutions and structures.

Of course, just as was the case for individuals, institutions live in the already/not yet paradox of our days. Notwithstanding the fact that they have been disarmed and defeated they continue to exert power and control. Often they continue to demand ultimate allegiance. Their ultimate and final dethroning is certain. In the meantime, however, they remain restless and prone to rebellion.

The role of Christians in business, then, is to reinforce the truth of Easter. The resurrection stands as a vital reminder that God has absolute authority, not the structures, institutions and worldviews of our day. These structures and institutions remain important. They were designed originally for the good of humanity. To achieve this good, however, they must return to their more modest, subservient roles for which they were originally intended.

Thus, a Christian can embrace free markets, capitalism and the institution of business as structures that can give order to God's world and provide a framework in which it can flourish. At the same time, anyone who lives this side of Easter must consistently affirm in word and deed that only God has the right to claim our ultimate allegiance, and that these structures and institutions deserve our respect and obedience only in their subordinate role. Put differently, the purpose of Christians in business is to serve their God and to do so by enabling their communities to flourish. Free markets and capitalism are to be affirmed insofar as they support and nurture this service. They are to be resisted when they seek to assert authority over and against the God who created them.

As Rebecca Blank, Undersecretary of Commerce for Economic Affairs in the Obama administration, has noted:

> The role of the church is not to be "anti-market" or "pro-market" but to be life-affirming. In cases in which markets and incentives promote better life opportunities, the church should affirm this, but when the

market limits opportunity and creates human misery, the church must call the market to judgment.[6]

## NEW HEAVEN AND NEW EARTH

If institutions are truly conceived of as mediating entities—that is, powers designed to hold back the chaos of the sea—it may well be that they will cease to have any use when New Jerusalem arrives. We are told that in the end "the sea will be no more," and in such a world dikes would have little value. We also have a couple of hints of a postinstitution world. Jesus notes that "at the resurrection people will neither marry nor be given in marriage" (Matthew 22:30), and in Revelation we are told that there will be no temple in New Jerusalem (Revelation 21:22). No families. No organized religion. It does not seem too far-fetched to imagine a world without other institutions as well, and specifically for our purposes, a world without capitalism, a market system, and other institutions of business.

But that remains for the future. For now, God has mercifully provided us with institutions to hold life and allow for its flourishing. If we can resist the call to treat them like gods, these institutions will enable God's kingdom work to advance as we live "between the finish lines."

---

[6]Rebecca Blank and William McGurn, *Is the Market Moral? A Dialogue on Religion, Economics and Justice* (Washington, D.C.: Brookings Institution Press, 2004), p. 53.

# 7

# How Then Should We Do Business?

So after all of this, where do we end up? Can we identify an overall framework to guide our approach to management? In light of the grand narrative of Scripture, how then should we do business?

Much of what has been said so far perhaps can be best summarized by asking and answering three questions.

- What is the proper purpose of business? To what end should a company be managed if it is to best glorify God?

  *Answer:* A business exists *to serve*.

- What are the appropriate limits of business practices? Assuming that a business should do all that it can to achieve its purpose, what constraints must it respect along the way?

  *Answer:* A business should seek to conduct its operations in a manner that is *sustainable*.

- Should business go it alone? What should be the posture of business toward other institutions?

  *Answer:* A business should work in concert with other institutions and seek *to support* them as they collectively pursue the common good.

## PURPOSE: TO SERVE

We begin with *purpose*. If we want to answer why business matters to

God, we have to start with understanding the role that God wants for-profit companies to play in our world.

Starting with the creation story, but continuing on through the final chapters of Revelation, we have identified the purpose of business as service. In particular, a business that seeks to glorify God should aim to serve in two ways: First, it should seek to provide the goods and services that a community needs to flourish (an external focus). Second, it should seek to provide opportunities for individuals to express aspects of their God-given identities through meaningful and creative work (an internal focus).

Moreover, what it means for a community to flourish has two foci. It has a creative, forward-looking piece: Is there an innovation, a new product, a new way of delivering a service, a new market that will help to bring a healthy, increasing abundance to the community? But it also has a restorative, redemptive perspective as well: Is there a product or service that can help address the broken relationships, the oppression and injustice in the world today? As Christians in business who are responding to both the creation and the redemption mandates, we are called to consider both perspectives.

Leaders in business are constantly called on to make decisions. These include internally focused decisions (How will we organize? Who will I hire? How will I finance my operations?) as well as decisions that are externally oriented (What should I make? Who should I sell it to? At what price?). In each case this model of purpose suggests that the question to be answered in making these decisions is not in the first instance, *Which decision will maximize my return on investment?* Rather, this model suggests that the corporate leader should first ask, *Given my core competencies and the assets under my control, how can I best deploy my resources to (1) enable this community to flourish, and (2) provide opportunities for my employees to engage in meaningful and creative work?* This is a very practical difference. This question is fundamentally different than those often asked in business, and if this becomes the defining frame of reference it will transform the way that much of business is carried out.

A couple of clarifying words about this purpose statement may be in order. First, this statement of purpose deliberately steers away from certain broader conventional statements of business purpose. For example, if the purpose statement was left as broad as "Business exists to serve the common good," it would be quite possible for some to argue that the shareholder-maximization model so dominant in the world today is simply an expression of this purpose. Similarly, the oft-repeated statement that business exists "to create wealth" would leave open the question of wealth for whom and how to create it. Again such a phrase is broad enough to allow for virtually any philosophy of business to be subsumed under its wings, including shareholder maximization, stakeholder balancing and other alternatives. The statement of purpose that I am advocating deliberately drills down to another layer to talk about the appropriate beneficiaries of the service and the ways they are to be served.

Second, remember that the purpose statement has been crafted to get at the intrinsic purpose of business activities as seen from God's perspective. This is not to demean the instrumental purposes of business. A person can engage in business activities to make money that can be used to feed his or her family and support missionaries, both noble and godly purposes. Focusing on instrumental values, however, just doesn't let us say much about the intrinsic value of the business activity itself. Money can be made by working in business, in government, for a church or for an NGO. The instrumental value that can come from the activity (i.e., the money that we earn and can use for good purposes) does not in and of itself render the underlying activity intrinsically meaningful. After all, even bank robbers can tithe. Our purpose throughout this discussion has been to consider what about the business activities themselves—buying, selling, hiring, shipping, financing, advertising, keeping of accounts—is pleasing to God.

Third, it is important to recognize that the range of possible decisions that could be made to pursue these purposes will inevitably be constrained by a variety of factors, including the need to provide shareholders with a reasonable rate of return on their investments. For example, even though a company might conclude that it could best enable a community to flourish by selling its products at below-cost prices, it should not do so. To do so would not be sustainable, and as will be discussed shortly, sustainable practices are also aspects of what it means to operate a business as God would like.[1]

---

[1]Helen Alford and Michael Naughton (*Managing as If Faith Mattered* [Notre Dame, Ind.: University of Notre Dame Press, 2001]) have developed one of the best comprehensive and systematic models for examining the purpose and practice of business through a Christian lens. Because many of my readers may be familiar with this work, I thought that it might be useful to compare their approach with the approach that I am advocating here. In many respects, the two models overlap. Indeed, I suspect that a business leader operating under the Alford and Naughton approach would be operating in a manner consistent with the approach I have advocated here and vice versa. The key differences appear to be in how the models are described.

First, Alford and Naughton draw implicitly, and in some cases explicitly, on Catholic social teaching to ground their approach. By contrast, I have attempted to ground my model in Scriptures. Given the congruence of Catholic social teaching and Scriptures, however, it should not be at all surprising that we have ended up in essentially the same place. It is probably worth noting as well that Alford and Naughton's development of the "common good model of the firm" is described largely in philosophical terms rather than specifically Christian terms. In an effort to encourage discussion and business practices in an increasingly global human community, Alford and Naughton note, "The model we present contains little that is specifically Christian, and so there is little that will impede dialogue or obstruct a practical consensus across religious lines. Such a dialogue and such a consensus must occur if we are to live in peace and flourish in the fast developing, one global community" (ibid., p. 42). While I too am interested in developing a model that will function effectively in the global community (and one that may have resonance with other faith traditions) the purpose of my book is different. I am writing to help Christians position and understand their daily work in business within their particular faith tradition.

Second, Alford and Naughton appear (although I would not insist on this too strongly) to have a more internal focus for the purpose of business. For them, business exists to promote "integral human development of each member of the firm" and the "communal development of the members of the firm, or community of work." In this respect their purpose is similar to my call for businesses to provide employees with meaningful and creative opportunities to express aspects of their God-given identities through work. It perhaps goes further than I do in emphasizing the fundamental purpose of community development (see chap. 1, n. 22). But it does not seem to go as far as I do in emphasizing an external focus. That is, it does not speak (at least at the level of purpose) in terms of the value of business in providing goods and services to enable the community as a whole to flourish. This is either not a piece of the ultimate purpose of business as construed by Alford and Naughton or at least not a purpose that is featured as strongly as I have in my model.

Third, we approach the need for profit differently, although again I suspect that our different models end up in the same place. Alford and Naughton speak of profit as a "foundational good." As such, it is a legitimate part of the firm's *purpose*. But it is only "foundational" and not one of the "excellent" goods that businesses should also pursue. The pursuit of foundational goods, such as profits, is important, but according to Alford and Naughton "must remain *a means to* and not the ultimate end of business activity" (ibid., p. 49). In effect, while profit is a legitimate goal or *purpose*, it is a subordinate one. It is to function as a means to the end of businesses' pursuit of the higher purposes of human and communal development.

In my model, I have found it more convenient to distinguish between purposes and constraints. I have suggested that a business has two overarching primary purposes: serve its com-

Fourth, note that this statement of purpose does not say that employees are to be favored in all respects over those who provide capital. It does not say, for example, that so long as a business can pay a reasonable rate of return to investors, any excess profits should be directed toward the employees. It does not say that the purpose of business is to pay the employees the most money possible or to provide products to the community as cheaply as possible. Indeed the *purpose statements* do not focus on the appropriate division of profits.[2] They focus on the kinds of goods and services that will be produced and the nature of the jobs being provided. To turn these statements into a blanket employee-first or customer-first approach to all business decisions would be to miss the point.

Fifth, note that these statements set forth what from God's perspective should be the inherent purposes for *all* businesses.[3] These purposes

---

munity by providing goods and services that will enable the community to flourish, and provide meaningful and creative jobs. I too recognize that profit is of critical importance and will necessarily occupy a great deal of management's attention. Management must pursue profit as the means necessary to ensure that it can pay an adequate return to shareholders and thereby attract the capital that it needs to pursue its legitimate purposes. Thus, just like Alford and Naughton, I believe that profit is a means to the ultimate end of the business. I simply find it conceptually more useful to think of the need to generate a reasonable profit not as an independent goal or purpose, but as a constraint. To me this serves the valuable function of continuing to highlight the real purpose of business (or what Alford and Naughton would describe as the "excellent goods" that business should ultimately be focusing on) and avoids the risk of sliding into a more traditional stakeholder analysis where everybody's "stake" is on the table and the manager is simply adjudicating between them.

As I have attempted to make clear elsewhere in the book, day-to-day management activities will often appear a lot like a juggling or balancing of competing demands. By separating purposes from constraints, however, I hope to highlight that all of that balancing and juggling is being done in service of the higher purposes. Conceptually, and in application, I doubt that there is much difference between the approach taken by Alford and Naughton and my approach on this point. Semantically, however, I have found the distinction between purpose and constraints to be useful.

[2]This doesn't mean, of course, that issues of fair pay are irrelevant to a faithful steward of God's business. Such questions are simply not addressed by a consideration of the proper *purpose* of business. They can raise serious ethical issues and often involve issues of justice. In the structure that I am proposing, however, these are issues more properly considered under the following section on limits.

[3]Of course, I'm under no illusion that everyone will choose to operate their businesses in the manner that I am advocating here. That doesn't negate God's intentions, however. God intends for each of us to love one another. The fact that we often don't doesn't change God's intentions or render them inapplicable to our lives. Similarly, these are normative purposes for businesses that Christians are called to pursue, and they remain God's call whether or not Christians (or, for that matter, non-Christians) choose to pursue them.

explain, in effect, why business matters to God. God's kingdom purposes are advanced when businesses pursue these objectives. Of course, particular businesses will also have their own individual statements of purpose or mission. Company-specific mission statements can give expression to particular aspects of these more generalized purposes. For example, a recycling business might exist for the purpose of protecting some aspect of the environment.[4] That specific mission statement would fit well under the broader statement of purpose advanced here even though I would not say that a foundational *purpose for all businesses* should be the protection of the environment.[5]

Finally, note that the purpose statements are intended to focus on the ultimate goal of the business, not just on a strategy. They are intended as expressions of why business exists and how business success should be measured. Often, when sharing these purpose statements with others, I run into business leaders who assure me that they already run their businesses by keeping a "keen focus on the customer" or by constantly seeking to "develop their talent." However, further conversations sometimes reveal that these approaches are really being viewed as tactics in pursuit of some other agenda. They are being pursued as strategies that will help the business succeed. When asked what business success means, the answer often comes back to more profits and more money for the shareholders. In other words, it is sometimes difficult to tell from the initial statements made by a manager (or sometimes even from a company's mission statement) whether a business is in business to serve or whether it simply views service as an effective tool for enhancing shareholder wealth. And the difference matters.[6]

---

[4]For example, the mission statement of ACM, a U.K.-based waste management company, includes the following purpose: "To make a positive difference by continuously offering waste solutions that reduce customers' carbon footprint, thus reducing global warming."

[5]Other company-specific missions include, "To unlock the potential of nature to improve the quality of life" (Archer Daniels Midland); "To help all people live healthy lives" (Becton, Dickinson); "To constantly improve what is essential to human progress by mastering science and technology" (Dow Chemical); to "clothe the world" (Levi Strauss); and "To nourish and delight everyone we serve" (Darden Restaurants).

[6]"Feldballe and other seekers are not like the business people who calculate economic purpose based purely on personal gain, *even though they may look the same on the surface in any one decision*" (Nash, *Believers in Business*, pp. 92-93, emphasis added). See the discussion of motivation in ibid., pp. 88-93.

Only when businesses are fulfilling their God-given purposes are they engaged in kingdom work. So it is important that we start with purpose—but of course we don't end there. Purpose must be joined with limits and set in the context of partnerships if business is to be truly all that it was designed to be.

## PRACTICE: SUSTAINABLE

Think of business like a mighty river racing down the hill toward the sea. Here the sea represents the purpose of business outlined earlier. It is the destination of the activity—what it is all aiming toward. If business is to be done right, the river must be directed toward the correct sea.

But simply having the correct purposes does not ensure that business will be done right. A mighty river not only needs to be sent to the correct destination. It also needs levies along its banks to keep it within its proper channels as it races downhill. Without the levies, the river will often spill over its banks and do harm to the surrounding countryside. Business is a huge and powerful institution in the world today, capable of much good. But without constraints, *even if it is pursuing appropriate ends*, it will still often spill over in damaging ways.

What are the appropriate constraints?

Earlier in the discussion of the Fall and its consequences, I noted that limits that inhered naturally in the goodness of the Garden were disrupted by human beings' unwillingness to live as limited creatures. Adam and Eve chose to disobey God in their desire to "be like God." Consequently, if we are now to participate in God's redemptive activities, that is, to participate in putting things right, we need to help redeem and restore these original limits. A full understanding of God's desires for business must include not only an understanding of what a business should do (its purpose) but also an understanding of what a business should not do (its limits).

One of the current business buzzwords is *sustainability*. Frequently, it is used in reference to the protection of the environment. To operate sustainably, a business should not operate in a manner that imposes costs on the earth and other natural resources if such costs could not be imposed forever, that is, if such costs exceed the "carrying capacity" of the environment. In this sense sustainability is a flexible version of the Hippocratic Oath for business. It requires that as businesses pursue their objectives, they should, at least over the long term, "do no harm."

As I discussed earlier in chapter two, however, the notion of sustainability is also sometimes used in a broader sense than solely in respect of environmentally neutral practices. And it is in this more comprehensive sense that I use it here. Shalom, as found in the Garden, was characterized by sustainable relationships across all dimensions. Not only did it provide for sustainable interactions with the created order but also for sustainable relationships between God and humanity, and between human beings.

In the context of business, then, the pursuit of purpose should be limited by the notion of sustainability. As business pursues even godly objectives, it should do no harm. And this do-no-harm constraint should apply to all of the business's stakeholders. It applies to investors who provide business capital and to employees who contribute their labor. It applies to suppliers who provide raw goods and to customers who purchase finished goods. It applies to the communities that nurture businesses and, of course, to the natural environment in which business is situated.

With respect to investors, sustainability requires that shareholders receive a reasonable, risk-adjusted return on their investment.[7] Perhaps it goes without saying, but obviously for a business to do no harm to investors it must operate at a profit. To use up capital without generating an adequate return is clearly not sustainable. Integrity, justice and respect require that investors receive what they have contracted for. Shareholders are also entitled to transparent and honest financial accounts and clear statements of management's philosophy and plans.

With respect to employees, sustainability means that their character as God's image-bearers cannot be used up. This requires that they be

---

[7]See Stephen N. Bretsen, "The Creation, the Kingdom of God, and a Theory of the Faithful Corporation," *Christian Scholar's Review* 38 (2008): 150, for a brief discussion of the difference between reasonable profit and maximized profit.

treated as having intrinsic value, not just as a means of production. It requires that their privacy be respected and that they not be required to work in conditions that are unreasonably dangerous or demeaning. Sustainability requires that businesses respect the rhythm of rest and work that God built into the fabric of his creation, a rhythm that is necessary to allow for right relations with God and for the full humanity of individuals. A 24/7 demand for workplace availability is not sustainable. The notion of sustainability also undergirds the notion that employees should be paid a living wage. It is not sustainable for a business to use up all of the productive capacity of a person and not give him or her an amount sufficient to live on in return.

Suppliers are also entitled to honest and transparent dealings. Moreover, they are entitled to respect as integral parts of the production process. Sharp dealings with suppliers or overly aggressive uses of market power to beat down supplier prices are not sustainable practices in the long term.

Customers are entitled to know what they are purchasing and entitled to products that meet their reasonable expectations for usefulness and safety. They are likewise entitled to fair prices. Deceptive sales practices and violations of consumer privacy infringe on the dignity of individuals made in the image of God. Marketing techniques that cultivate an insatiable consumerism are by definition creating a condition that is nonsustainable, a condition of constant dissatisfaction, a condition that is never at equilibrium, a condition that is always seeking "just a little bit more."

Communities must also be dealt with in a sustainable fashion. Communities provide much of the legal, social, aesthetic and intellectual capital that businesses require to thrive. Don Flow, the owner of a number of car dealerships in the Southeast, recently noted:

> But we know that there is much more than economic capital needed for flourishing—there is aesthetic capital, intellectual capital, political capital, and social capital as well. And while business focuses on economic capital, it draws on all of the others. For example, economic capital will not grow without social capital, since trust is required for transactions to

take place. . . . Perhaps we should now better understand the role of business as a part of a larger system, and recognize business should not exist that destroys other kinds of capital as well.[8]

A number of years ago, a wealthy private investor adopted a business plan of buying up regional beer companies. He would purchase them on the basis of their going concern value, capitalizing their projected future income stream. Since advertising plays a significant role in building market share for beer companies, each of the companies that he purchased had spent and planned to continue spending considerable amounts on marketing its products. The projected cost of continued advertising substantially reduced the projected income stream and was included in the calculations used to establish the purchase price.

Once the purchase of a company was completed, however, the investor immediately terminated all advertising. Without this expense his short-term profits were substantially increased. Over a number of months this investor effectively drained off the company's good will. When sales decreased to the point that it was no longer profitable to operate the business, the investor closed the factory and sold off the assets. The effect of this was to secure for the investor very substantial returns on his initial investment but to impose substantial costs on the community where the company had operated. From the standpoint of the community's "capital," this was an unsustainable business model. The investor took but did not give back.

Four related observations about sustainability:

On this side of New Jerusalem we live in the messy middle. What this means is that full shalom-sustainability remains to some extent an aspiration. It is one thing to say that these are limits that will prevail when "the earth will be full of the knowledge of the LORD as the waters cover the sea" (Isaiah 11:9). It is quite another to say that they can be fully imposed here and now. In light of the fact that we still live in a fallen world, it may not always be possible for a business to operate fully within these constraints. It may not be possible to earn a reasonable return for inves-

---

[8]Don Flow, "Maintaining Ethics in a Downturn: Auto Sales," interviewed by Al Erisman, *Ethix* 64 (2009): 9.

tors and pay all employees a livable wage. It may not be possible to continue to provide jobs that a community relies on and avoid all adverse long-term effects on the environment. It may not be possible to ensure suppliers with pricing sufficient to keep them afloat and avoid advertising that is designed to stimulate a previously unknown consumer appetite. In short, as we wait, work and long for God's kingdom to be fully realized in our midst, there may not be enough to go around.

What then does this mean for those of us in business? Put simply, we pray, we orient our businesses toward God's purposes, and we strain to live within these limits as best we can.

A second observation is a corollary to this first one. Much of the tactical, day-to-day operations of a business necessarily involve balancing competing demands. Can the business afford more investment in research and development right now in hopes of securing a product that will enable a community to flourish, or must it scale back in order to improve the ROI for investors? Can the business afford to increase salaries for its lowest-paid workers above a living-wage threshold and still keep product prices in line with those of its competitors? Can the business afford to make an additional capital investment in equipment with a smaller carbon footprint, or should these funds be directed toward ensuring a better pricing policy for suppliers? And so on.

In this balancing it will often be appropriate to prioritize the need for a reasonable return on investment for investors over other constraints. This is not because shareholders as a class are inherently entitled to more deference than other stakeholders. Rather it is because profitability (at least over the long term) is a necessary prerequisite to the continuance of the business, which in turn is a necessary prerequisite to dealing sustainably with other stakeholders.

It is certainly conceivable that there may be occasions when a company should forgo being profitable for the sake of staying true to kingdom values. Jesus' obedience to the Father led him to the cross, not to worldly success. This would suggest that even survival as a business must not be the ultimate litmus test. It may be that sometimes the cost of survival in ethical terms is just too high. But this call to business martyrdom surely must be the rare case. In general, if a company is to be a tool in God's hands for human flourishing, it must stay in business.

Which leads to a third observation. The mere fact that a reasonable rate of return for shareholders is a first-order constraint does not convert it into a purpose. Consider an analogy. If the survival of a particular retail business was dependent on being able to continue to lease space in a particular location, this would make timely payment of the rent a very high priority. It would not however, make payment of rent the underlying purpose of the business. The business would not exist for the sake of the landlord. Similarly, while paying a reasonable risk-adjusted return to shareholders remains critically important for the survival of the business, it does not mean that this is why the business exists. From God's perspective the business exists to serve—by providing the goods and services that will enable the community to flourish, and by providing jobs that allow employees to engage in meaningful and creative work. As blood is to a body, so profit is essential to a healthy business. But no mentally healthy person lives for blood.

One last observation. The very reason the business exists is to pursue its purpose of service—but the sustainability limits will often seem much more visible, insistent and urgent. Particularly, the focus on sustaining profitability can be very intense. In this environment it is far too easy for management to lose sight of the overarching purpose of the organization. As Alford and Naughton put it:

> Thus, sound management *involves planning and organizing for the promotion of [the organization's highest purposes]*, as an integral part of the business operation. The competitive market environment guarantees that the pursuit of [profits and other foundational goods] nearly always seems urgent. *Attention to [the highest purposes] must, therefore, be deliberate and sustained* in season and out, lest the management's attention simply give way.[9]

If we are to effectively steward God's business, we will need to keep God's purposes always before us.

---

[9]Alford and Naughton, *Managing as If Faith Mattered*, p. 45, emphasis added.

## PARTNERSHIP: SUPPORT

Earlier, I suggested that certain aspects of the creation mandate could be best pursued through business activities. In particular, business creates wealth. It makes things, and it makes things better. In Genesis parlance it helps enable the land to "be fruitful," to "fill the earth." Business is also well situated to provide organized opportunities for meaningful and creative work.

Of course there are other aspects of the creation mandate that can be best advanced by nonbusiness institutions, such as family, government or education. In a manner roughly analogous to the use of the "body metaphor" by Paul in the New Testament, I suggested that different institutions have different strengths and abilities, and are best deployed to focus on the fulfillment of certain aspects of the creation mandate. And of course, the same is true of the call to participate in God's work of redemption.

But here it is important to remember another aspect of Paul's body analogy. So far I have used this analogy to emphasize the point that different institutions can have different callings. Paul, however, uses the metaphor primarily to emphasize the opposite perspective—that is, that while there are many parts, they are all one body. By extension, the purpose of business ultimately cannot be conceived of in isolation. It is one institution among many, one part of a whole.

Business in the twenty-first century is well suited for certain responsibilities. Other institutions are better suited for others objectives. Together, however, they serve the common good. Or hearkening back to the discussion of the powers, business is not *the* dike that holds back chaos. It is one part of *a system of dikes* that collectively does this work.

What does this mean then for the practice of business?

At a minimum, it means that business leaders need to respect the authority and responsibilities of other institutions. For example, business leaders should not assume that the metrics and language of their discipline will be appropriate for other institutions. Efficiency is the language of the market place. It may not be appropriate, however, for aspects of family life, education, religion and government. Very few of us would seek to justify bedtime stories with our children using a cost-benefit analysis. Nor should we. Criminal procedure, with its due process, its presumptions of innocence, its juries and appellate courts, could hardly be defended on the grounds of efficiency. Rather it seeks to advance the values of equality, fairness and justice—values that do and should inhere in a criminal justice system but which often make such a system woefully unproductive and from some perspectives wasteful.

Respect also means that business leaders need to work hard not to take advantage of weaknesses that may crop up from time to time in other institutions. Businesses need to respect appropriate institutional boundaries even where such boundaries are not well defended. For example, even where local labor markets give employers the upper hand—that is, when jobs are at a premium—business managers should not overwork their employees to the detriment of the employees' family lives. Even where the enactment and enforcement of environmental and labor laws in developing world countries is lax, a business should not take advantage of these gaps to lower its costs of production if doing so would result in serious damage to the local environment or the inhumane treatment of its work force. And even though some government officials may be highly susceptible to being influenced by campaign contributions and other corporate perks, a business should take care not to use its economic muscle to undercut justice or to subvert government's proper role as a neutral umpire on the field of economic competition.

In each case respect for other institutions is grounded on the conviction that all institutions are intended by God to work together to seek the common good. When a business takes advantage of another weaker institution, it may be able to advance its own parochial interests, but it will do so only at the cost of the whole. It may win its individual battle, but it will contribute to losing the war.

But partnering for the common good ought to lead businesses beyond a mere avoidance of trespassing to a more active support for the work of other institutions. There are many instances where such support from business will allow the institutions to accomplish more together than either could accomplish on its own.

Of course, the notion of businesses partnering with other institutions is nothing new. There are literally hundreds of examples of such arrangements. For example, businesses have frequently worked with local governments to strengthen the cultural and aesthetic life of the community by providing leaders for local arts boards and funding for significant projects. In many cities United Way draws on business leaders to provide leadership and direction for campaigns that have raised millions of dollars to strengthen the safety net for some of society's most vulnerable members. Educational institutions have routinely partnered with businesses to secure funding and materials for basic research in science and engineering. Governments have worked closely with businesses on trade missions to help nurture the economic health of the community. Many NGOs are now regularly working with businesses to establish and monitor standards designed to address issues such as global climate change, human rights, endangered species or local cultural resources. Many businesses provide day care facilities and other so-called family-friendly benefits to nurture the family life of their employees. And so on.

But in spite of this long track record, proposed partnerships between businesses and other institutions are often initially met with a high degree of skepticism. And this is particularly true with respect to arrangements involving the government.

From my experience Christians in business, as a group, are no more friendly to government regulations than business persons in general. In virtually every case, government activity is characterized as "government interference" that will only end up throwing sand in the cogs of the market machinery. In my conversations with Christian business leaders I have rarely heard anyone suggest that business should support a more active role for government. Inevitably, less government is characterized as better government.

From a biblical perspective, of course, much of this skepticism about government is certainly warranted. After all, governments, like business, operate post-Fall, and it is easy to identify many instances of even well-motivated government actions that in retrospect ended up doing more harm than good. Nonetheless, the knee-jerk antagonism to any form of government involvement strikes me as growing out of a business worldview that fails to fully appreciate the biblical understanding of institutions. Different institutions were intended by God to support one another as together they collectively pursued the common good.

One place in particular where Christians in business might welcome more, rather than less, government regulation is in settings where the government could help level the playing field. By raising standards across the board, government regulation might allow a Christian who felt compelled to honor higher standards to continue to effectively compete in the marketplace.

For example, suppose that a Christian manager concluded that it was contrary to God's desires for the environment for him to continue to dispose of a particular toxin by dispersing it into the air. Assume that under the current law he would be allowed to do so and that this is the waste-disposal approach that all of his competitors utilize. Suppose also that it would be very expensive to treat the waste in a more environmentally sensitive fashion.

What should he do? If he continues to pollute, he does so in violation of his Christian convictions. If he acts unilaterally to dispose of the waste in a more environmentally sensitive fashion, he will be operating at an extreme competitive disadvantage. But what if he joins forces with a local environmental group to persuade the appropriate governmental authorities that air-borne disposal of the toxin should be banned? If he is successful, he will be able to remain in business and compete on an even footing with others in the industry. The environment will be protected not only from the damaging disposal of waste from his production facilities but also from the facilities of his competitors. And he will be able to move forward with a clean conscience. Why would a Christian in business not welcome government regulation under such a circumstance?

But there is an even deeper reason that Christians in business should embrace a more healthy partnership with government. Put simply, left to its own devices, business will fail. It simply lacks the internal mechanisms needed to keep it away from destructive excesses.

This has become abundantly clear in light of the recent collapse of the subprime mortgage market. Reflecting on the economic meltdown, Alan Greenspan, former head of the Federal Reserve Bank and a leading proponent of a relatively unregulated free market, remarked, "I made a mistake in presuming that the self-interest of organizations, specifically banks and others, were such that they were best capable of protecting their own shareholders and their equity in the firms." He expressed shock that this "central pillar to market competition" should break down.[10]

The Caux Round Table, an advocacy group focused on improving the way business is conducted, added:

> To put it bluntly, the so called immune system of laissez-faire market discipline failed to control the speculation. . . . The one positive that we can take out of all this is that it has finally shattered the naïve belief that "unfettered" financial liberalization . . . can be a path to securing sustainable economic prosperity and social progress.[11]

As a consequence of the collapse, public trust (which is so critical to the health of business) has dipped to historic lows. According to the Edelman 2009 Trust Barometer, less than half of the global public now trusts business to do what is right, and the number is closer to a third in the United States.[12] By a three-to-one margin, the public believes that more regulation is needed.

And indeed, government regulation is needed, but not because business is bad or driven by voracious greed. Government involvement is needed because business was never designed to function alone. It is a reflection of the idolatry of our age that we have been lulled into believing that the market—left alone—would deliver on the promise of shalom. "Laissez-faire has proven an unreliable guide for aligning the in-

---

[10]Alan Greenspan, comments made at the hearing "The Financial Crisis and the Role of Federal Regulators" held by the House of Representatives Committee on Oversight and Government Reform, October 23, 2008.

[11]Noel Purcell, "Repairing Capitalism's Immune System," *Caux Round Table*, June 30, 2009 <www.cauxroundtable.org/newsmaster.cfm?&menuid=99&action=view&retrieveid=28>.

[12]"2009 Edelman Trust Barometer," Eddleman <www.edelman.co.uk/files/trust-barometer -2009.pdf>.

terests of business with those of the larger society."[13] The institution of business is only one part of a system of dikes that were designed *collectively* to promote the common good. Business needs government (and of course, government needs business).

## SUMMARY

In summary, then, business managers should orient their companies to serve. They should seek to provide the goods and services that will best enable their communities to flourish and to structure their workplaces so as to afford their employees with opportunities to engage in meaningful and creative work. As they pursue these twin goals, they should seek to do so within the limits of sustainability. That is, their choices should be constrained by the need to operate as much as possible in ways that "do no harm" to any of their stakeholders, including shareholders, employees, customers, suppliers, environment and community. In particular, except in the rarest of cases, a Christian's business decisions must always take into account the need to pay a reasonable, risk-adjusted return on invested capital. And as the business pursues its purposes, it should always do so mindful of the fact that it was designed to work in partnership with all other institutions so that collectively they might advance God's kingdom agenda here on earth. To this end, business managers should operate their businesses in a manner that respects other institutional agendas and where possible looks for opportunities to collaborate in a synergistic fashion to advance the common good.

---

[13]Daniel Yankelovich, *Profit with Honor* (New Haven, Conn.: Yale University Press, 2006), p. 87.

# 8

# Making It Real

## A FEW FINAL QUESTIONS

I have had the privilege of sharing many of the thoughts in this book with different groups—with Christians and non-Christians, academicians and practitioners, theologians and business leaders. And while I have been somewhat surprised by the enthusiastic reception that these ideas have generally received, I am also aware that there are often some lingering questions. Indeed, many of the same questions show up time and again.

So, I want to finish with a brief look at the concerns that are most commonly raised. You might imagine that in this last chapter you are watching a question-and-answer session that comes at the conclusion of my prepared remarks. My hope is that this back-and-forth will help dispel any remaining sense of "Yeah, but . . ."

### WHAT ABOUT PROFIT?

This question often comes cloaked with "Aw, come on." "Aw come on. You are the dean of a business school for goodness sake. Do you mean to tell me that your school doesn't teach about profit or return on investment?"

Of course we do. We offer a fairly conventional business program that covers all of the traditional topics: management, marketing, finance, information systems, accounting and the like. And throughout we are concerned with helping our students develop the skills they will need to run efficient and profitable businesses. But there is one difference. We do not teach profit (or for that matter, return on investment or earnings per share) as the ultimate goal of the endeavor. Rather we teach it as a means to the end. Profit is critically important to a business because it is the means of attracting the capital that a business needs in order to do what it should be doing in the first place, which is to serve.

Consider the analogy of a not-for-profit organization. Suppose, for example, that you were to ask the executive director of a large organization such as the American Lung Association why her organization exists. Would it not strike you as strange if she responded that her organization exists to raise funds? Surely you would expect that instead she would say something like, "The organization exists for the purpose of promoting scientific research for curing lung disease." You might then ask a second question: "What do you spend most of your time doing?" "Oh," she would respond, "We spend most of our time trying to raise funds."

The same is true for business. It exists to serve—to serve by providing goods and services that enable the community to flourish and to serve by providing its employees with meaningful and creative jobs. What do business leaders spend most of their time doing? Focusing intently on the bottom line. Profit is not easy to come by, and generating profit is critical to the health of the organization. It just isn't the purpose—the why—of the business.

In the final analysis profit is also not a measure of the success of a business. As I've argued earlier, market forces are not necessarily aligned with God's kingdom values. There may be times when Christians in business are called to make decisions that will make their businesses less competitive in the marketplace for the sake of the gospel. In those cases the more successful business (at least measured against the scale of what God would want the business to be) might be the less profitable one.

Similarly, profit is not a reward. If there is no necessary alignment between obedience to God and the profitability of the business, it is difficult to understand how business profits could be characterized as a reward for right behavior. Moreover, it is a dubious theology that suggests right behavior will be validated or rewarded with material success. After all, Jesus' obedience was "rewarded" with the cross.

If then profit is not the purpose of a business, not the measure of business success, and not a reward for right behavior, what is it?

As I have already stated, at a minimum, profit, or more accurately a reasonable risk-adjusted rate of return, is the quid pro quo *offered to shareholders* in exchange for the investment of their capital. Unless the business is profitable (or anticipated to be profitable), it will not be able to secure the capital that it needs to survive. In this sense, profit is the means by which capital is attracted into the business.

The need for profits also imposes limits on the choices that a business might otherwise make. I have already talked about profit as *a constraint*. For example, a business manager might want to give her employees more paid time off, sell her products for a lower price and make sizable donations to local charities. In some respects all of these options might better enable her community to flourish. But so long as this business manager also needs to generate a profit, she may not be able to do all that she would want to. The need to be profitable narrows and constrains the range of possible decisions.

But profit is more than this. It is also a *measure*—if not of the ultimate success of the business, of at least of one key indicator about the business. How efficiently is the business being run? How closely is the business aligned with applicable market forces? To say that alignment with market forces will not assure that the business is pursuing kingdom values does not mean that the extent of alignment with market forces is unimportant. Market forces are powerful and will over time dictate which businesses survive. Even though there may be instances where a business owner will need to sail deliberately into the headwinds of the market, he should do so with eyes wide open. Tracking profitability enables the business owner to locate the business in the context of the pushes and pulls of the marketplace.

And profitability is even more than this. Profit, or more accurately the need to ensure that the business turns a profit, is actually a *powerful tool* that will often help a business achieve its mission of service. It forces managers to bring a laser-like focus to distinguish between what is important and what is not. It helps ensure that resources are deployed in ways that are optimally efficient. Potential is not wasted and mediocrity is not accepted. In short, pursuit of profit can be a powerful accelerant in the pursuit of mission—at least most of the time.

Consider another analogy. A friend of mine coaches high school basketball.[1] If you ask him what his goal as a coach is, he will tell you that it is to develop character in the young men he works with. Not winning, but character development.

If we watched a practice before the season started, however, we might be surprised. He has the team running lines until they are drenched and physically too drained to move. He has the team shoot literally hundreds of free throws. He regularly dresses down players who forget their assignments, but saves his worst tongue lashings for players who are giving less than 100 percent to the drills. And if anything, the intensity goes up in games. He shouts. He gets in his players faces. He cheers and jumps, pumping his fists with enthusiasm. He throws down his note pad in disgust. He paces. He screams. One thing is absolutely clear: he wants very badly to win.

When I point out his passion for winning and suggest that it seems at odds with his stated goal of character development, he seems confused. He doesn't see a contradiction. Indeed, he points out that he couldn't develop character in his players without an intense focus on winning. It is precisely as his players learn to invest deeply in a common goal, to play as a team, to work hard for something that may or may not come in the future that character is formed. Unless winning is pursued as if a goal, none of the character lessons could be taught.[2]

Of course, not all coaches are like my friend. I'm quite sure that many of them don't actually care about character formation and really

---

[1]This again is a composite story, and I am grateful to my friends Barry Rowan and Jeff Pinneo for this analogy.
[2]This may be close to what Bill Pollard means when he refers to profit as a "means goal" for his company (William Pollard, *Serving Two Masters? Reflections on God and Profit* (New York: HarperCollins, 2006), pp. 2-4.

are all about winning. And here's the thing. Most of the time as we watch them, we won't be able to tell them apart from my friend. Both seem to be doing all they can for a victory. But sometimes, at the edges, the differences are revealed.

From time to time one of my friend's players falls behind in his studies or gets caught drinking at the school dance or skips a class or two. Many other coaches would likely overlook such minor infractions for the sake of winning the game. With my friend, however, there is no question about what will happen. Even if the player is the team star, and even if the game is for the championship, the player will not suit up. He will not play. Why? Because my friend truly believes that it really is all about character formation. Most of the time going all out to win nurtures the development of character. Sometimes, however, winning needs to take a back seat because going for the win would get in the way of character formation.

It's a lot like that with profit in business. It is not the ultimate goal, but it can be a marvelous tool that brings forth the best from the company. It disciplines the organization. It enables the organization to create value. More things and better things are made for less. In many ways it is the engine that drives the purpose forward. Just as with my friend's approach to basketball, however, from time to time profit-seeking will need to take a back seat to the ultimate mission of the organization. Business is not ultimately about winning. It's about service.

One of the central contentions of this book is that from God's perspective the dominant paradigm of the purpose of business currently embraced in most of the world needs to be turned on its head. Instead of customers and employees being means of serving shareholders, shareholders and their capital should serve customers and employees. In making this claim as strongly as I can, however, I risk falling into an opposite trap. I risk creating the impression that profit is unimportant, easy to secure or, worst of all, somehow slightly sordid. I mean none of these things. Those who scorn profit-seeking are scorning one of the more effective tools that can be used to provide for God's children and advance God's kingdom. My only point is that it is a tool, not a destination.

## WHAT ABOUT SHAREHOLDERS?

Assume that I give you $50 to buy some books for me. You take my money and agree to make the purchase. Once I have given you my money, however, you decide that it would be better to spend the money on school supplies for underprivileged children. You buy pencils, paper and backpacks, but no books for me. Do I have a right to complain?

Of course I do. In philosophical (and legal) terms you have violated your duty as my agent. It doesn't matter that you didn't use the money to enrich yourself or that you did a good thing with the money. It was my money, and you didn't use it as I directed and as you agreed you would.

The question about shareholders raises important agency concerns. In one form or another the person raising this question is usually asserting that shareholders have given management their money with the understanding that management will deploy the invested funds so as to maximize the returns for shareholders. If this is a true statement of the relationship, wouldn't using the funds to serve customers and employees be a breach of a manager's duties as an agent?

This is indeed a difficult question and I want to propose a number of possible responses.

*Easy cases.* First, there are many easy cases. If the shareholder/owner is also the one running the business, as is the case with many small and medium size businesses, there is no tension. In effect, the principal and agent are collapsed into one.

Alternatively, if the charter of the company (or statements of management) makes clear *before funds are invested* that any contributed capital will not be used in the first instance to try to maximize ROI, the shareholders who invest thereafter should be understood as doing so with a clear understanding of the arrangement. They have no standing to complain that management is not respecting any contrary desires that they might have for their investments. For example, when Google first went public, its SEC filing contained a letter from its founders that stated: "Eric, Sergey and I intend to operate Google differently, applying the values it has developed as a private company to its future as a public company."[3] Google's website continues to state expressly that it will subordinate potential increases in shareholder value to a commitment to ensure the best possible service to its users.[4] Anyone investing in Google has no basis to complain—no agency argument—about Google's failure always to seek to maximize ROI.[5]

Another easy case occurs when management legitimately believes that there is no conflict between pursuing service—and specifically the service to customers and employees I have advocated for here—and maximizing the return to investors. In such a case of happy coincidence there is no conflict and no basis for shareholder complaints.

But these are the easy cases. And even though they probably represent the vast majority of situations, we still need to look at the hard cases.

**Hard cases.** What about a situation where a shareholder is investing in a company that he is not managing and that has not expressed an intent to be governed by an alternative approach? In that context, can the management pursue any strategy other than maximizing ROI without running afoul of its duties as an agent for the shareholders? What can we say in this situation?

There are three possible ways of responding—all of which are helpful, but none of which is wholly satisfying. First, we could reasonably ask whether most shareholders are really "principals" entitled to assert a principal-agent relationship. Second, we could raise questions about the content of the charge to the agent. And finally, we might ask

---

[3]"Letter from the Founders" as set forth in amendment no. 9 to form S-1 Registration Statement, filed by Google, Inc., with the Securities and Exchange Commission on August 18, 2004.

[4]"Our Philosophy—Ten Things We Know to Be True," *Google*, September 2009 <www.google.com/intl/en/corporate/tenthings.html>.

[5]Another example of a "disclaimer" statement of management philosophy can be found in the initial public offering statements for AES, a global energy company. In his book *Joy at Work*, Dennis Bakke includes the text of a paragraph from the draft of the initial public-offering memo sent to the SEC: "An important element of AES is its commitment to four major 'shared' values. . . . AES believes that earning a fair profit is an important result of providing a quality product to its customers. However, if the company perceives a conflict between these values and profits, the company will try to adhere to its values—even though doing so might result in diminished profits or forgone opportunities. Moreover, the company seeks to adhere to these values not as a means to achieve economic success, but because adherence is a worthwhile goal in and of itself" (Dennis Bakke, *Joy at Work* [Seattle: Pearson Venture Group, 2005], pp. 38-39).

whether higher values, in effect, trump the duty of management to be faithful agents.

*First response.* No one would argue that investors who offer uncovered puts and calls on stocks are principals entitled to complain about management actions. They are pure speculators—not investors. None of their money ever goes to the company. They might as well be betting on who will win the Oscar for Best Picture. If, contrary to their bets, the management of a particular company takes action that reduces the company's share price, the speculators may lose, but they can't legally (or philosophically or morally) bring a claim against management. Management simply owed them no duty.

Now most investors today, particularly investors in public corporations, bear much resemblance to these speculators. They are almost never giving any money to the company. Only in the case of new stock offerings, which are fairly rare, are shareholders actually investing new money into the company. Rather, most persons buying shares of company stock are giving their money to another shareholder—not investing with management at all. Moreover, like those speculators who offer puts and calls, most investors are buying stock only in the hope that it will appreciate in value so that they can sell it at a profit. They are betting, in effect, that the company's financial prospects will improve. Often they have little or no interest in what the company actually does—just in whether its share price is going up. In short, we might argue that these types of investors are entitled to no more deference than are speculators in the options market.

*Second response.* But assume for the moment that this argument does not satisfy you. After all, shareholders, unlike pure speculators, are at least stepping into the shoes of someone who did invest money in the company, albeit often many times removed. The next line of inquiry then would focus on the nature of the charge the shareholder-principal ostensibly gives to the management-agent when he or she invests funds.[6] Of

---

[6]We could argue that the only charge worth considering is the charge given by the shareholder who originally purchased at the IPO. All the subsequent shareholders take derivatively and arguably can only assert, at best, the charge of the original investor. This would tend to further

course, no one really sends in their money with a letter directing that the funds be used to maximize returns. In fact, there are no explicit instructions that accompany a stock purchase. Whatever charge is being given to the agent is implied either in law or in custom, and it turns out that both are murky and migrating.

Under the "Model Business Corporation Act," which informs the legislation governing businesses in most states, management is charged with acting in a manner that it "reasonably believes to be in the best interests of the corporation." The content of this phrase has received clarification in the courts, and most famously it has been interpreted as meaning "in the best interests of the shareholders."[7] But this case precedent is old and has been challenged and ignored on many occasions.[8] Moreover there are recent examples to the contrary. In addition, a large majority of state codes now contain so-called other-constituency provisions that explicitly authorize management (at least in certain circumstances) to consider the interests not just of shareholders but of other stakeholders as well.[9] As law tends to do, it is changing with underlying societal expectations, and there can be no doubt that much of society is moving away from a strict expectation that all management decisions be made to maximize returns for shareholders.[10]

---

mitigate the agency concerns since the expectation that management will always seek to maximize ROI is a relatively recent phenomenon (see Allan A. Kennedy, *The End of Shareholder Value: Corporations at the Crossroad* [Cambridge, Mass.: Perseus, 2000], pp. 1-2, 33-45).

[7]*Dodge v. Ford Motor Company*, 204 Mich. 459, 170 N.W. 668. (Mich. 1919).

[8]Richard Marens and Andrew Wicks argue persuasively that *Dodge* does not require shareholder maximizing behavior on the part of management. Indeed after surveying the law, they conclude that in "the corporate setting, fiduciary duties do not impose a requirement that a business be run in a certain manner. No court equates this duty with 'maximizing shareholder value' even assuming such an indeterminate concept could be estimated" (Richard Marens and Andrew Wicks, "Getting Real: Stakeholder Theory, Managerial Practice, and the General Irrelevance of Fiduciary Duties Owed to Shareholders," *Business Ethics Quarterly* 9 [1999]: 277).

[9]For a discussion of these provisions see Marjorie Kelly, *The Divine Right of Capital: Dethroning the Corporate Aristocracy* (San Francisco: Berrett-Koehler, 2001), pp. 137-41.

[10]I don't mean to underemphasize the potential legal difficulties. There are some who continue to believe that the law precludes management from operating a company for any purpose other than maximizing shareholder wealth. See for example, Joel Bakan, *The Corporation* (New York: Free Press, 2004), p. 37. This has led others to work for revisions to laws to create "a new legal structure for companies eager to embrace broad social commitments without fear of recourse from disgruntled shareholders" (G. Jeffrey MacDonald, "When 'B' Means Better: 'B Corporation' Status Reveals Commitment to Benefiting Others," *Christian Science Monitor*, July 22, 2009, p. 14).

In a recent global survey of senior level corporate executives, McKinsey & Company found the following:

> Unquestionably, the global business community has embraced the idea that it plays a wider role in society. More than four out of five respondents agree that generating high returns for investors should be accompanied by broader contributions to the public good—for example, providing good jobs, making philanthropic donations, and going beyond legal requirements to minimize pollution and other negative effects of business. Only one in six agrees with the thesis, famously advanced by Nobel laureate Milton Friedman, that high returns should be a corporation's sole focus.[11]

Of course this is not the same thing as the service model advocated here, but it does undercut the claims of shareholders that profit maximization is a well-understood and implied charge to management that accompanies every stock purchase. Arguably the charge to the agent from the investor principal is sufficiently general as to allow for the adoption of the approach advocated here without violating any duties management owes to its shareholders.

*Third response.* Finally, one further argument might be asserted. In law there is a concept referred to as *ultra vires*, which literally means "beyond powers" and is invoked from time to time when someone claims that a corporation is attempting to take an action beyond the specific powers granted to it in its charter.

Perhaps we could make a parallel argument with respect to a shareholder's investment in a company. If we start with the assumption that all assets are owned, in effect, in trust for God, then we could conclude that an investor does not have unfettered power to dispose of assets however she sees fit. The investor must use them in conformity with the will of the creator of the trust (i.e., God) because she merely holds them in trust and does not own them outright. If so, were an investor to give instructions that the assets should be used in

---

[11]"The McKinsey Global Survey of Business Executives: Business and Society," *McKinsey Quarterly*, January 2006 <www.mckinseyquarterly.com/The_McKinsey_Global_Survey_of_Business_Executives__Business_and_Society_1741#>.

a manner inconsistent with the trust arrangement (i.e., contrary to God's will), then the investor arguably would be acting beyond her powers. Put differently, we might argue that the investor lacks the power to direct management to use the assets in a manner inconsistent with God's intent. If God wants the assets of business deployed to serve customers and employees, a manager might argue that he is free to ignore contrary instructions from the shareholder on the grounds that the contrary instructions are beyond the authority of the shareholder in her capacity as trustee.

Of course, there are some obvious problems with this line of reasoning as well. If carried to an extreme, it would do away with the notion of agency altogether. Agents could always substitute their understanding of God's will for that of their principals. But perhaps in this more limited setting of remote shareholders and murky investor expectations, the *ultra vires* argument should be given some weight.

In any event, while there are some arguments that could be made, none of them conclusively addresses the agency concerns in the hard case. But there is a way out, actually a very simple solution. Previously, I have suggested that if the company's charter explains that the company will not pursue a profit maximization model, shareholders who choose to invest in such a corporation would have no basis for complaining when the company did what it said it would.

Nearly the same result can be achieved even if investors have already invested in a business. A business manager who wants to run the business in accordance with the service-model advocated here should clearly and publicly announce his intent to do so. Since the shareholders always retain the right to remove a manager, their acquiescence in the face of such an announcement would amount to an acceptance of the manager's construction of their agency relationship. The manager would be declaring, in effect, that if he is given the opportunity to do so, he will treat the agency relationship as one that allows him to direct the company in pursuit of service to customers and employees. It is then up to the shareholders to decide if this is the kind of relationship that they want to govern their investments.

## CAN THIS APPROACH TO BUSINESS REALLY WORK?

Underneath this question is usually the concern that the market may not tolerate a business that operates in the manner I am advocating. If a business pursues the first-order goals of providing quality goods and services and meaningful and creative jobs, if it limits itself by principles of sustainability (even where it is not legally required to do so), and if it seeks to support the work of other institutions rather than capitalizing on their weaknesses, will it be competitive? What will happen to its cost structure? What about its cost of capital? Isn't this just a recipe for business failure?[12]

I always want to be careful about how I answer this question. I do not want to suggest that this model of business should be adopted because "it works." It is not being proposed as a tactic. Rather, business should be pursued as I have outlined here because it would be right to do so. Doing so aligns the business with God's values and plans. As I have noted before, I also do not want to suggest that good ethics is always good business. Faithful discipleship in business will not invariably redound to a stronger bottom line. "The practical point to be drawn from these reflections is not that honesty always pays off; it does not. It often has costs. For moral reasons alone, these costs are worth paying."[13]

Having said this, however, I do believe that adopting the approach outlined here is likely to prove *highly* competitive in today's marketplace for a number of reasons. First, societies around the world are already expecting more of business than just maximizing returns or increasing share value.[14] A business that aligns its performance with society's ex-

---

[12]This is essentially the argument advanced by Robert Reich in his book *Supercapitalism*. Reich argues that in the hyper-competitive global market in which businesses must compete in the twenty-first century, there is little to no room for corporations to act socially responsible unless the so-called socially responsible behavior is really the best strategic option for minimizing costs and maximizing margins. "Companies under supercapitalism no longer have the discretion to be virtuous. Competition is so intense that most corporations can not accomplish social ends without imposing a cost on to consumers or investors—who would then seek and find better deals elsewhere" (Robert Reich, *Supercapitalism: The Transformation of Business, Democracy and Everyday Life* [New York: Alfred A. Knopf, 2007], p. 173).

[13]Michael Novak, *Business as a Calling* (New York: Free Press, 1996), p. 168.

[14]There are a number of reasons to anticipate an increasingly hospitable reception in the general

pectations should expect to see higher sales, lower transaction costs and lower costs of capital.

And we can find hints of this in many contexts. The willingness of some consumers to pay more for "shade-grown, free trade" coffee beans—which taste exactly like all other coffee beans from the same region—hints at the value consumers may be willing to place on so-

---

business community to the model that I am advocating here. As noted in chap. 8, n. 11, the McKinsey survey of senior executives underscores the broadening international expectations for business. This may be in part because international expectations of business have always had more of a communitarian flavor than has been the case in the highly individualistic practice of business in the United States. As U.S. businesses become more global, they are finding that it is increasingly necessary to consider societal values that go beyond the company's financial bottom line. But it no doubt has also been fueled by the series of recent scandals. The dominant shareholder maximization model, while perhaps not the direct cause of many of these failures, has nonetheless proven to be very dry fodder that easily bursts into flames in the face of unethical sparks. There seems to be a growing recognition that market forces, in and of themselves, are insufficient to produce right behavior.

Other factors that may make the adoption of the model I have proposed less controversial include the growing corporate social responsibility (CSR) movement, the adoption of the United Nations' Global Compact and its related work on business and human rights, and the growing interest in social ventures and social entrepreneurship. While none of these developments maps directly onto the model I am promoting here, the trend in society's expectations of business that these developments reflect suggests that in general those seeking to implement a stewardship model may find an increasingly hospitable climate in which to do so.

Marc Gunther, an editor for Fortune magazine, identifies a number of companies who are approaching business differently. "More than that, though, they want to rethink the very purpose of business. The purpose of business, they argue, is not to generate profit. The purpose of a business is to better the lives of the people it touches—and to serve the common good. . . . These changes are not disconnected. Taken together, *they add up to nothing less than a quiet revolution that has begun to transform corporate America.* Big companies are gradually remaking themselves so they can do more to serve the common good. . . . To be sure, only a Pollyanna would say that all companies are changing this way. . . . *But I have come to believe that most companies, like the ones in this book, are moving toward a more humane vision of what business should be*" (Marc Gunther, *Faith and Fortune: The Quiet Revolution to Reform American Business* [New York: Crown Business, 2004], pp. 10-11, 28). William Greider says, "My premise—that American capitalism is ripe for reinvention—is not based on a fanciful supposition. The most compelling reason for expecting deep reform is the new circumstance described [earlier]—the paradox of secure abundance accompanied by the stressed social reality" (William Greider, *Soul of Capitalism: Opening Paths to a Moral Economy* [New York: Simon & Schuster, 2004], p. 25). Bo Burlingham adds, "The shareholders who own the businesses in this book have other, non-financial priorities in addition to their financial objectives. Not that they don't want to earn a good return on their investment, but it's not their only goal, or even necessarily the paramount goal" (Bo Burlingham, *Small Giants: Companies That Choose to Be Great Instead of Big* [New York: Portfolio, 2005], p. xvii). And Daniel Yankelovich says, "I suspect that companies will gradually shift away from giving shareholders top priority" (Daniel Yankelovich, *Profit with Honor* [New Haven, Conn.: Yale University Press, 2006], p. 130).

cially responsible practices. The growth in socially responsible mutual funds highlights the value some investors are willing to assign to good corporate behavior. The fact that a number of major corporations have begun to pay attention to issues of climate change—not just as public relations initiatives but as components of their core business strategies—likewise suggests that businesses are finding themselves needing to respond to and align with a broader range of expectations.

Similarly, one ought to expect that companies that are passionate about serving their customers will develop significant brand loyalty and see an increase in sales. Customers can tell when they are being cared for and when they are being marketed to. In the first case they are the ultimate object of the company's efforts. In the second they are merely a means to an end.

Perhaps the best argument for the competitiveness of the service approach, however, is linked to employee motivation. In this twenty-first-century knowledge-based economy, many of the most important assets of a business often cannot be found on its balance sheet. Rather, in many cases the wealth of the company, that is, its capacity to generate high returns, will be embedded in the creativity, knowledge, talent and relationships of its employees.[15]

> Talent is the scarce resource because it is the ultimate generator of the intangibles that drive the creation of wealth in the digital age. Winning companies are those that can increase their profit per employee by mobilizing labor, capital and mind power into profitable institutional skills, intellectual property, networks and brands.[16]

How then can employee energy and creativity best be released? Imagine trying to motivate employees by reminding them that this is all about

---

[15]This may be particularly true given the changing nature of the U.S. workforce. Daniel Yankelovich notes that the long-term trend for the United States shows a steady increase in the number of jobs requiring high levels of discretion and extra initiative. According to his figures, "high-discretion" jobs made up only 18 percent of the jobs prior to World War II. By 2000 that number had risen to 62 percent. "Our competitive success in the global economy does not depend solely on capital and technology; it depends critically on employee morale and commitment" (Yankelovich, *Profit with Honor*, p. 112).

[16]Lowell L. Bryan and Claudia I. Joyce, "Better Strategy Through Organizational Design," *McKinsey Quarterly*, no. 2 (2007): 24.

maximizing the return for shareholders. Explain to them that they should give every last ounce of their energy and creativity to the company so that the company and its owners can make more money. Alternatively, imagine helping them understand how their work connects to solving a problem in their community, or brings opportunities to segments of society who have previously been underserved, or makes advances in human health possible, or brings beauty to places of ugliness, or allows for access to new information, or, more generally, how their work is producing goods and services that will enable their community to flourish. Which seems most likely to unleash their best efforts?

In a 2004 interview with *Fortune* magazine, Jeff Immelt, CEO of General Electric said this:

> To be a great company today . . . you also have to be a good company. The reason people come to work for GE . . . is that they want to be about something that is bigger than themselves. They . . . want to work for a company that makes a difference, a company that's doing great things in the world.[17]

Bill Pollard, the retired CEO of ServiceMaster, tells the story of Shirley, who was a ServiceMaster employee working as a housekeeper in a 250-bed community hospital. After fifteen years on the job she still seemed excited about her work, and Pollard wondered why. Day after day she mopped and wiped and cleaned the same floors, the same rooms, the same toilets. "The dirt has not changed nor have the unexpected spills of the patients or the arrogance of some physicians."[18] The answer, Pollard discovered, was that Shirley had come to see her work in terms of the mission of the hospital. "She has a cause."[19] She was not just cleaning floors. She was an integral part of the team that was bringing healing to the sick. She was about something bigger than herself, something bigger than the economic well-being of ServiceMaster.

---

[17]Marc Gunther, "Money and Morals at GE," *Fortune* 150 (2004): 176.

[18]C. William Pollard, *The Soul of the Firm* (New York: HarperBusiness, 1996), p. 46.

[19]"Every firm should be able to articulate a mission that reaches beyond the task and provides a hope that the efforts and activities of its people are adding up to something significant—so significant, in fact, that even more can be accomplished than is expected" (ibid.).

Indeed, she was about the work of the kingdom.

In short, it seems logical to suppose that the service model advocated here has a better chance than the profit-maximization model of connecting with employees in ways that will inspire and motivate them to bring their best to the workplace.

This observation has found some empirical support in the work of Jim Collins and Jerry Porras. In their book *Built to Last*, Collins and Porras identify eighteen pairs of companies, each in a different industry. One company in each pair was labeled "visionary" and the other "good," in each case based on long-term financial performance. According to the authors the visionary companies were like the gold-medal winners and the good comparison companies were the silver-medal runner-ups. The authors then asked if there were any common factors that tended to distinguish visionary companies from their industry counterparts.

It turns out that one factor related to the organization's understanding of its purpose. Indeed this factor was found to apply in seventeen of the eighteen pairs, and was one of the clearest differences that the authors identified.

> Contrary to the business school doctrine, we did not find "maximizing shareholder wealth" or "profit maximization" as the dominant driving force or primary objective through the history of most of the visionary companies. . . . Through the history of the most visionary companies we saw a core ideology that transcended purely economic considerations.[20]

Put simply, the most financially successful companies were the ones that did not view the purpose of business as simply maximizing shareholder ROI.

To illustrate this point, Collins and Porras quote Henry Ford, founder of the Ford Motor Company:

> I don't believe we should make such an awful profit on our cars. A reasonable profit is right, but not too much. I hold that it is better to sell a large number of cars at a reasonably small profit. . . . I hold this because

---

[20]James C. Collins and Jerry I. Porras, *Built to Last* (New York: HarperBusiness Essentials, 2002), p. 55.

it enables a larger number of people to buy and enjoy the use of a car and because it gives a larger number of men employment at good wages. Those are the two aims I have in life.[21]

David Packard, cofounder of Hewlett Packard, says:

> Why are we here? . . . You look around [in the general business world] and still see people who are interested in money and nothing else, but the underlying drives come largely from a desire to do something else— to make a product—to give a service. . . . The real reason for our existence is that we provide something which is unique [that makes a contribution]. . . .
>
> Profit is not the proper end and aim of management—it is what makes all of the proper ends and aims possible.[22]

I am not suggesting that any of these companies currently operate under or were even founded on precisely the service model that I am advocating. I would suggest, however, that these are just a few examples of many companies who have been very financially successful even while pursuing a business purpose that subordinates profit maximization to some broader goal. In short, to answer the question at hand, there is ample reason to believe that this model can and will work in the marketplace.

## WHAT SHOULD I DO WHEN I CAN'T HAVE IT ALL?

Managing a business is all about making decisions. Of course, not all decisions raise ethical issues. Some are merely tactical. A supplier wants to sell me socks at $.50 a pair with net 15 payment terms. I offer to buy the socks at $.40 a pair with payment terms of net 30. We settle on a sale price of $.50 a pair and payment terms of net 30. Both parties to this transaction had to compromise to make the deal, but this was not a compromise that touched ethical concerns.

Other decisions do raise ethical issues. In many cases, however,

---

[21]Henry Ford, quoted in ibid., p. 53.
[22]David Packard, quoted in ibid., p. 56. Collins and Porras find similar sentiments expressed by George Merck II (Merck), Masaru Ibuka (Sony), Robert Johnson (Johnson & Johnson) and a number of others (ibid., pp. 46-79).

these are not difficult to resolve. Where I am already making a reasonable rate of return on my investment, should I sharply drive down my employees' wages to a standard well below a living wage in order to allow me to make more money? Should I increase my profits by running a misleading ad campaign? Should I save money by disposing of toxic waste in an unsafe manner? Here, the ethical answers are clear. (Of course, this does not always make me do the right thing. Competitiveness and greed may tempt me to choose the unethical path. It's just that it is not that difficult to determine where the right path leads to.)

When I hear the "What if I can't have it all" question, however, it is usually not in reference to these kinds of business decisions. Usually the inquiry is asking a more difficult question. Specifically, what should a manager do when she cannot pursue godly purposes for her business and, at the same time, operate within the limits of sustainability? As discussed previously, the call to sustainability remains aspirational. Some day it will be possible to pursue godly purposes and do so in a way that always avoids harming anyone. For now, however, we must practice business in the messy middle. The kingdom of God is already here but not yet fully consummated; we live in the midst of this already/not yet paradox.

What if stopping production of a product that is proving harmful to society would make it impossible for a company to pay a reasonable rate of return to its investors? What if there is no way to organize the jobs that need to be done in order to secure the production that the company needs and at the same time allow its employees to express their creative instincts? What if the company cannot simultaneously pay a livable wage to its employees and a reasonable rate of return to its investors? What should a manager do when he concludes that his manufacturing processes cannot be reconfigured to protect the environment and at the same time allow his business to stay profitable? How should he decide what to do? Or, putting it bluntly, at least as measured against the standards of the kingdom of God, who should he shortchange?

Here we come to the truly difficult ethical issues, the "borderline situations."[23] These are situations where the choice to uphold one kingdom value *necessarily* requires that I come up short on another. What if I can't have it all?

In the face of this question the only authentic response is silence. There is no answer that can be given, no "three easy steps" to resolving these dilemmas. In a way, these decisions can only be made by living into them. Indeed, any effort to give rules in advance ultimately becomes an obstacle to what God intends as Spirit-informed improvisation in the moment. In one sense all that we can say is that as we listen the Spirit will guide.

It is, however, possible to suggest certain practices that may make us more receptive to the work of the Spirit in these moments. Recall the parable of the Sower of the Seeds (Mark 4:1-9). In this story the ultimate harvest is not dependent on the quality of the seed. The same seed is sown everywhere. Fruitfulness turns on the *preexisting condition* of the ground where the seed lands. While we cannot presume to know what seeds will be sown, we can (with God's help) till our ground to help prepare us to receive the Spirit's guidance. Let me suggest a few of these ground-tilling guidelines:

***Stay alert.*** First, it often takes practice and spiritual sensitivity to spot the tensions when they do arise. Many Christians in business tell me that they rarely experience the market-kingdom tension that I am referring to here. And while there are a number of reasons why this may be so, no doubt prominent among them is the impact of cognitive dissonance.[24]

> Christians in business regularly align their behavior with market forces. They are trained to do so, they are rewarded for doing it well, and they are severely punished when they fail to do so. Given that this

---

[23]For a discussion of the meaning and analysis of the borderline situation, see Helmut Thielicke, *Theological Ethics*, ed. William H. Lazareth, 3 vols. (Philadelphia: Fortress, 1966), 1:578-608.

[24]I have discussed this phenomenon and possible explanations at greater length in Jeff Van Duzer, "Free Markets and the Reign of God: Identifying Potential Conflicts," in *Global Neighbors: Christian Faith and Moral Obligation in Today's Economy*, ed. Douglas A. Hicks and Mark Valeri (Grand Rapids: Eerdmans, 2008), pp. 109-32.

is deeply entrenched behavior, it is not surprising that Christians in business should find it difficult to accept that this behavior may in some sense be violating their deeply held religious beliefs. Dissonance theory accurately predicts that they will tend to explain away any apparent inconsistencies.[25]

In the midst of the hectic demands of running a business, it is easy to miss market-kingdom conflicts. Christians need to build in regular times of prayerful reflection on their work in order to remain spiritually sensitive to these dilemmas.

***Don't readily conclude that there is no way out.*** If, on the one hand, there is a tendency to miss these tensions altogether, there is a corresponding temptation when we do encounter them to too quickly throw up our hands and claim that there is no way out. "I had no choice. In order to meet my customer's deadlines I had to push my employees beyond reasonable limits and insist that they work in unsafe conditions. There was no way that I could continue to operate my business profitably given the demands of the marketplace and simultaneously pay proper concerns to the welfare of my workforce. I was stuck."

Christians must resist the temptation to come to this conclusion any sooner than they absolutely have to. These seeming tensions must first drive Christians to turn over every stone in search of a third way. One of the skills that business leaders are best known for is their inclination to pursue, and their capacity to find, win-win solutions. This must be all the more true of Christians in business. Often what seem like inevitable tradeoffs can, in fact, be avoided with a mixture of diligent looking and creative thinking.

***Practice praying in the moment.*** If there appears to be no way out, prayer in the moment is critical. Since resolving these tensions is necessarily an act of improvisation, Christians must seek the guidance of the Spirit.

Theologian and ethicist Helmut Thielicke has argued that this failure to turn to God in the moment may explain why the priest and the Levite passed by their beaten neighbor in the parable of the good Sa-

---

[25]Ibid., p. 114.

maritan (Luke 10:30-37).[26] As Thielicke explains, the priest and Levite may have attempted to resolve the tension posed by the bloodied man on the side of the road through rational assessments, that is, by weighing the claim of a prior commitment against the claim of the moment. "Thus improvisation was hampered by calculation."[27] Or, Thielicke suggests, they may have never carefully reflected in advance of this encounter on the question of their duty to neighbors in need. In the absence of such reflection they may have allowed anxiety and a desire for self-preservation to control their decision. "In either case the Spirit, who is bent upon action, was given no room to operate."[28]

I know that one of my consistent failures in the face of ethical tensions is to assume that somehow determining the correct resolution is up to me. Sometimes I will simply turn away and choose to ignore the dilemma. Other times I will engage in a careful mental calculation designed to arrive at the most loving course of action. In either case, I often forget to pray.

### Build long-term habits of the heart.

> We have much to say about this, but it is hard to explain because you are slow to learn. In fact, though by this time you ought to be teachers, you need someone to teach you the elementary truths of God's word all over again. You need milk, not solid food! Anyone who lives on milk, being still an infant, is not acquainted with the teaching about righteousness. But solid food is for the mature, *who by constant use have trained themselves to distinguish good from evil.* (Hebrews 5:11-14, emphasis added)

Christians in business need to train themselves through constant practices to discern right from wrong. They need to build long-term habits of the heart. This is to be done, in large part, through the cultivation of spiritual disciplines. These practices have been taught by the church throughout its history and include such things as daily prayer, fasting, keeping the sabbath, Scripture study, meditating on Scripture, practicing hospitality, living simply, practicing generosity, regularly

---

[26]Thielicke, *Theological Ethics*, pp. 652-53.
[27]Ibid., p. 653.
[28]Ibid.

participating in corporate worship and receiving the Eucharist. These practices need to be cultivated. Disciplined work is needed to turn these into spiritual habits, natural inclinations. They do not make God act any more than raising the sails on a boat causes the boat to move. But they do make us ready to receive the wind of the Spirit when it "blows wherever it pleases" (John 3:8).

*Live in community.* Christians are called to community. The decision to follow Christ is simultaneously a decision to be part of the church. The two are inseparable. Even though we so often live independently and seemingly self-sufficiently, this was never God's intention —nor even an accurate expression of the true spiritual reality.[29]

As Scriptures attest, community can be a source of comfort, support, accountability and grace. Perhaps most important for our purposes, it is also a setting in which God's intentions can be discerned collectively. Christians generally, and Christians in business in particular, should seek out small groups of fellow Christians who will commit to gather regularly, to care for and love one another, to hold one another accountable, and to seek God's will together.

I know of many such groups and many Christians in business who are in such groups. I wonder, however, how often business dilemmas are brought up in these settings for collective prayer and discernment. It seems to be easier for many of us to share concerns about our families and our prayer lives than about our jobs. This may be in part because the latter will take more explaining, but I suspect that it also reflects what is still a deep-seated, secular-sacred divide: "A small group can help me find God's will for my church life, but business decisions are up to me." Of course, as I have emphasized in this book, from God's perspective all of our lives are lived on holy ground. The body of Christ can help me discern God's will not only on "spiritual" questions but also on questions dealing with layoffs and acquisitions, advertising campaigns and contract

---

[29]"We are members of a body, not only when we choose to be, but in our whole existence. Every member serves the whole body, either to its health or to its destruction. *This is no mere theory; it is a spiritual reality*" (Dietrich Bonhoeffer, *Life Together* [New York: Harper & Row, 1954], p. 89, emphasis added).

negotiations. The prayerfully informed wisdom of others is often a much-neglected resource in business decision making.[30]

***Renew your mind.*** After eleven lengthy chapters of theology in the book of Romans, Paul turns to application. In light of all that has been said about God and his plans for the world, how then should Christians live? What does this all of this mean for Christians who are seeking to be faithful disciples? To answer these questions Paul identifies a number of specific directions in chapters 12–15. But before doing so, he sets out an overarching concept: "Do not conform any longer to the pattern of this world, but be transformed by the renewing of your mind. Then you will be able to test and approve what God's will is—his good, pleasing and perfect will" (Romans 12:2).

This is critically important for Christians in business. There are many well-established ways of thinking about business—patterns of this world—that we often accept as base-line assumptions not even worth a conscious thought. But as Christians in business we need to be "transformed by the renewing of our minds." Specifically, we need to immerse ourselves in Scripture. We need to be willing to bring all of the often unchecked first-order assumptions that we have been building our lives on into contact with Scripture. We need to study Scripture. We need to read it devotionally. We need to interact with other Christians around Scripture—and, in particular, to listen to Christians who live most of their lives grounded in other institutions and other cultures, and who bring different perspectives to the Scripture and its possible application to business. We need to learn to think biblically if we are going to adequately till the ground and rightly receive God's calling to us.

***Confess and long.*** Someday it will be possible to practice business in a way that completely honors all commitments, fully respects the dignity of all persons and always nurtures the goodness of creation. Paraphrasing the prophet Isaiah, someday suppliers will live with customers and investors will lie down with lenders, the environment and the busi-

---

[30]See a general discussion of the role of small groups for many Christian CEOs in Laura Nash, *Believers in Business* (Nashville: Thomas Nelson, 1994), pp. 186-93.

ness will dwell together in shalom "and a little child will lead them" (Isaiah 11:6). In the end, these conflicts and tensions will disappear.

But not yet. In the meantime we are called to make our decisions humbly and in a spirit of confession and longing. Even as we end up choosing one kingdom value over another, we cannot escape the fact that we are participating in work that falls short of the glory of God. We have failed—albeit perhaps unavoidably—to live signs of God's coming kingdom into this world. And so we confess.

We also long. As we reflect on God's assurance that there will come a day when all of this will be behind us, we can allow these promises to nurture a powerful longing in us. Over and over we can join in the great final prayer of Scripture, "Maranatha. Come Lord Jesus." This is not a debilitating longing that leaves us wistfully looking at the clouds. It is a longing that grows into such a powerful desire that we can do nothing other than roll up our sleeves and jump in, hoping in some small way to hasten the coming of that wonderful day. So we confess and we long.

## HOW CAN I DO BUSINESS THIS WAY?

This question is most often raised by recent graduates, and it is usually expressed as some variation of the following: "Someday, perhaps, I will be the president of a company. When I am in charge I can try to run the business in accordance with God's designs. But right now I am heading into an entry-level position within a giant organization that appears aligned from top to bottom around the goal of profit maximization. What relevance is any of this to me?"

A fair question indeed. Why bother with all of this if it only applies to senior executives and folks who own their own businesses?

Here is how I respond. First, not all companies are created equal. Some seek to serve the broader community. Some provide opportunities for their employees to exercise creativity and engage in meaningful work. Some insist on conducting their business through sustainable practices. Others do not. At least with larger public companies it is often easy to locate mission statements, business case studies, newspaper articles and other sources of information that can help a prospective employee gain information about the company's culture in advance of signing on. Similarly, if the prospective employee has had an internship with the company or has friends or other contacts who work there, he or she can often find out a good deal about the character of the organization and about the way it is likely to approach future decisions. Armed with this information, prospective employees can vote with their feet. In short, one way to apply the business model that I am urging here is to choose to work for companies that value service over profit maximization and insist on sustainable business practices.

Of course, in a tight labor market a person might not always have such a choice. Moreover, for many private or smaller companies it may be difficult to tell in advance much about the corporate culture. What if an individual finds him- or herself in an entry-level position in a company with a different set of values?

There are, of course, aspects of ethical behavior that are always applicable regardless of the limits of one's responsibility and authority. At a minimum Christians in business should conduct themselves with integrity. They should insist on being law-abiding and seek to comply with all applicable company policies. They should be hard working, giving an honest day's work for an honest day's wage. Christians should be kind and compassionate to coworkers, avoid gossip and be generous of spirit in dealings with others. To the extent it is up to them, they should conduct their business in a way that does not inflict harm on others. Christians should work for the best interest of their company and community rather than focusing just on their own personal advancement. They should be humble, good listeners and eager to learn. All of these traits and more honor God and can be put into practice regardless of one's status within the company.

But what about the macrolevel issues of business purpose and practice that have been the focus of this book? How do new employees pursue this approach to business from the bottom of the corporate pyramid? The simple answer is that they pray and then do what they can within the circle of influence that they have been given.

Early on in an individual's career this circle can be quite small, perhaps no more than a few feet in diameter.[31] Over time, however, the
circle often grows. The employee may soon be leading a small team or
be in charge of a small piece of a bigger project. In every case, he or she
can ask how to do the assigned job in a way that best serves the team:
"How can I help design and structure jobs (and job requirements) to
increase the opportunities that my colleagues and I will have to engage
in meaningful and creative work?"

In small circles one typically will have only occasional and minor
opportunities to influence the corporate culture—but rarely are there
no such opportunities. This is not an all-or-nothing proposition: either
you are the president and can direct the whole organization or you can
do nothing at all. In small circles we can develop the posture of consistently leaning into service, and as our circle expands our influence on
the organization and its direction will grow.

Imagine, for example, that you have been working for two years for
a large manufacturing company. You have done well and are now the
leader of a team of three. Your team is responsible for selecting and
securing the pallets that are used in shipping your company's products
overseas. There is really not too much to the job. You regularly call for
bids from three companies that you have used for years. You pick the
lowest-priced option. You process the shipping and delivery documents.
You coordinate the inspection of the delivered pallets and make appropriate arrangements to secure adjustments for defects. The work is remarkably monotonous.

You could do as your predecessors have done: work hard to make

---

[31]Don Flow tells a wonderful story of a woman who bagged groceries for over fifteen years in
the same grocery store. She committed to pray for each person who would come through her
line and often inquired about them. Shoppers began to feel themselves strangely attracted
to her—so much so that it became a problem for the store as long lines would form at her
checkout station. She retired and died shortly thereafter. Contrary to what one might typically
expect, this funeral of a bag lady was packed with people who came to tell stories of how she
had touched their lives, how she had pastored them. According to Flow, this woman simply
said, "I'm going to claim the six feet that God has given me in my life. I'm going to reclaim
those six feet for Jesus Christ and I'm going to incarnate his ministry right here" (Don Flow,
KIROs annual dinner, Seattle, April 12, 2005).

sure the system runs smoothly, emphasize standardization and predictability with your team, and hope you get promoted to something more interesting soon.

Or you could lean into the possibilities raised by the business-as-service model. Suppose, for example, that one evening you take your team out to dinner and invite them to brainstorm about what could be done to improve the nature of the service that you are providing. One of them suggests that longer-term bids might minimize some of the busy work and still secure good prices. Another asks whether you might check out more about the suppliers. What if one of them has an exemplary record for good treatment of its employees and for the protection of the environment? You might want to favor this company—at least at the margins—in the bidding process. Still another wonders aloud about the use of so much wood. There might be pallets that are constructed from other materials that would mimic the strength of the wood but would be lighter (and therefore cheaper) and perhaps even be fully recyclable.

At the end of the evening each of you leaves with a charge to pursue one of these lines of inquiry. Although this involves additional work, the opportunity to research these options actually seems to energize the team. At the end of the process you locate a fourth provider who makes recyclable cardboard pallets and who has also recently been written up as one of the best places to work in the region. You shift some of your orders to this provider. The savings on shipping costs attributable to the lighter pallets are noticed by one of your superiors and your team is held up as a model within the company of how creative thinking can produce win-win solutions. Other groups in the firm begin to hold their own dinner meetings.

A bit far-fetched? Not really. While not every endeavor will be this successful or have this level of influence within the company, there are opportunities for service and sustainability lurking in almost every circle of influence. The key is to form the habit of looking for these opportunities and to lean into them whenever we are given the chance to do so.

## WILL ADOPTING THIS BUSINESS-AS-SERVICE MODEL MAKE ANY DIFFERENCE?

"Given that under the business-and-service approach that I am proposing, a company will be constrained by the need to secure sufficient profits to pay a reasonable return to investors, don't the profit-maximizing
strategy and the service strategy end up in the same place? In other words,
won't the uncompromising shackles of the market end up requiring the
company to make the same decisions under either model?"

In a word, no.

Neo-classical economics suggests that in a world of perfect information and complete rationality no company could continue to exist unless
it ruthlessly pursued business practices that kept its costs to the absolute
minimum, secured the highest price for its products that the market
would bear, and at all times returned the maximum possible amount to
its investors. A failure in any of these particulars would lead rapidly to
its demise. In such a world the profit-maximizing model and the service model would indeed take a business to exactly the same place.

But there is no such world. The market is often more like a loose-
fitting coat than a straightjacket.[32] As behavioral economists have been
arguing for years, imperfections in information and economically irra-
tional decisions abound. Ask the many companies who are expressly pursuing a stakeholder approach to managing their businesses. They will
attest that it is quite possible to run a business in a manner that rejects the
primacy of shareholder returns and still be quite financially successful.[33]

---

[32]"Not all companies chose the low road to solve the cost-price problems of intense competition.
Many large and small firms resisted and prospered nonetheless. Whether this choice reflected
the personal values of managers and owners or simply smarter business strategies, their success
did hint that *there is much more space for successful alternatives, even in the global context, than the
stern sermonizers of the free-market culture are willing to acknowledge*" (William Greider, *The Soul
of Capitalism* [New York: Simon & Schuster, 2003], pp. 37-38, emphasis added).

[33]Of course market limitations will vary by industry. In a commodity market where the means
of production are well established and uniformly used throughout the industry (e.g., steel) the
market will constrain the available choices more than it would in a boutique luxury market
(e.g., espresso drinks). But even in the tightest markets there will always be room to look for
opportunities to serve and to lean into sustainability. Frankly, if a Christian is ever found in
a business where the market constraints are so tight as to not allow him or her to make any
choices that differ from those being made by competitors, I would question why this person
thinks God has called him or her to that industry. If every person in this position, Christian or

I am not suggesting that operations under the two different models will look different in every case. There will be, of course, a substantial overlap between decisions made under the service approach and those made under the more traditional approach of profit maximization. This is true for a number of reasons. First, the need to be profitable will indeed constrain the range of options that one might otherwise consider under the service approach. Second, in many cases a profit-seeking discipline can actually enhance the capacity of the organization to serve. And third, pursuing an approach that seeks to serve the community and one's employees is quite often a pathway to enhanced profitability. That is, for some serving may be the ultimate purpose of their enterprise. For others service may be merely a tactic in aid of the goal of making more money. From the outside, however, both may often look the same.[34]

But at the margins and over time these two approaches will take business to different places. Fundamentally, they are asking different questions. Under one approach, the manager asks, "What decision should I make to generate the most money and maximize the return for

---

non-Christian, well intentioned or otherwise, would end up having to make exactly the same choice when confronted with a particular situation, is this really the best place to practice a life of discipleship? Wouldn't God's kingdom be better off if the person were to use his or her gifts and abilities in an industry where they might make a difference? But this is truly a theoretical concern. To my knowledge, there are no such truly straightjacket industries.

[34]Consider the case of Costco Wholesale Corporation. Costco has a stated policy of promoting from within and of paying all of its workers substantially more than true market wages. It also has a stated policy of capping its margins so that even when market conditions would allow it to increase its prices substantially, it declines to do so. It follows these practices in accordance with its statement of values that prioritizes service to employees and customers over returns to shareholders. But is Costco a model of the service approach? I don't know. It may genuinely be pursuing these objectives as the ultimate purposes of its business, or it may just have hit on a clever strategy for increasing its share price. (In general, Costco's shares have done well in the market.) From the outside it is simply too hard to tell. I have met and talked with Jim Sinegal, the cofounder of Costco. I am inclined to believe that the company is pursuing service as its ultimate objective rather than as a tactic, but it is not easy to say for certain. Consider the following quote: "Our mission is to do four essential things: obey the law . . . take care of our customers . . . take care of our people . . . and respect our suppliers. If we do these four things, and do them consistently, we will succeed as a business enterprise that is profitable and rewarding to our shareholders" (Al Erisman and David Gill, "A Long-Term Business Perspective in a Short-Term World," an interview with James Sinegal, *Ethix* 28 [2003]: 6-7).

my shareholders?" Under the other approach, the manager asks, "How can I best deploy the assets and core competencies under my control—in a sustainable manner and in concert with other institutions—to best serve my community?"

We do not need to look far to find examples of where this would have made a difference. What if, in the early 2000s, mortgage brokers had not been asking how they could make the most money? What if instead they had asked whether putting individuals into mortgages that they could not afford so they could buy houses that were beyond their means would truly lead to a flourishing community? What if companies using supply chains to manufacture goods overseas were not asking how to squeeze every last penny out of the process but were instead asking how they could structure the jobs in these supplier companies to affirm the dignity of the workers and tap into their creativity? What if companies were not asking how much waste could be legally dumped into nearby waterways but rather how to process the waste from operations so that over the long term it does minimal harm to the environment?

Different questions will produce different answers. And the differences matter a great deal.

■  ■  ■

In his book *The Dangerous Act of Worship*, Mark Labberton worries that the church in America has gone to sleep. "Not dead. Not necessarily having trouble breathing. But asleep."[35] It is not always obvious to us that this is so. We seem busy. Our lives are full—often with activities that we enjoy. But still much of the time we are sleepwalking, going through the motions. In quiet moments, if we are honest, we occasionally wonder if any of this really matters anyhow. Have we somewhere along the line exchanged adventure and what really matters for something else, for comfort, for the opportunity to stay busy?

A few pages back, I argued that creativity in the workplace could be unleashed if employees could be helped to understand their work

---

[35]Mark Labberton, *The Dangerous Act of Worship* (Downers Grove, Ill.: InterVarsity Press, 2007), p. 14.

in terms of the larger mission of the company. Imagine, then, what could happen if Christians in business began to wake up, to understand their work in terms of the largest mission of all, the work of the kingdom. What might happen if Christians in business understood their day-to-day work—analyzing spreadsheets, making sales calls, preparing a branding campaign, purchasing supplies, tracking inventory—as God's work? Work that contributes to the call that God gave to his people at creation. Work that has a part in God's ministry of reconciliation.

For far too long many Christians in business have accepted without challenge the notion that their work has only instrumental value. It may give them a platform to share their faith. It may allow them to earn an income and possibly make a little extra to give to the church. But if pressed, many Christians in business would have difficulty saying why God might be interested in the actual work they are doing. At best, such work is neutral. It has no intrinsic meaning. A good Christian faithfully observes a life of personal piety (don't lie, don't steal, don't cheat) in the workplace but finds meaning—purpose as a Christian—elsewhere.

But we need to wake up. We need to turn up the alarms, to sound the trumpets. The call to business is not neutral. It is not meaningless. It is a noble calling—a calling to participate at the very heart of God's work in the world. It is a calling to serve as God's hands and feet in feeding a hungry world and in bringing healing to the broken. It is an invitation to be commissioned as God's agents to further God's desire for human flourishing everywhere. And it comes with a reminder that the work we do in business matters *now*. It is part of the future kingdom breaking into the present reality. And it comes with a reminder that this work will matter for eternity—that in some mysterious fashion God will redeem our work and mold it into the new heaven and the new earth. A calling to business is a calling to work for God, who in the end will prevail. It is work with a purpose, work with hope.

The world is desperately waiting for Christians in business to wake up. Huge problems abound. Over 20 percent of the world's population

lives in extreme poverty, surviving (or not) on less than $1.25 a day.[36]
Over twenty-five thousand children under five die *every day*, mostly
from preventable causes.[37] Whole continents are ravaged by AIDS and
other epidemics. The natural processes of our earth are being over-
whelmed. Water is running out. Climate temperatures are climbing.
Hatred and ethnic violence are on the rise.

These problems are huge, too big for any one institution to solve. The
United Nations can't do it. Governments can't do it. NGOs can't do it.
Without the commitment of business, these problems will continue to
fester. And as long as Christians in business limit their understanding of
purpose to an enhanced bottom line and choose to leave these problems
to someone else, they will continue to lack this commitment.

But it need not be so. What if business leaders everywhere began to
ask how they could profitably direct the economic might of their organizations toward helping solve the truly big problems of our day? What
if in humility these business leaders partnered with leaders from other
institutions to better understand the nature of the problems and the
nuances of the needed solutions, and then joined forces to bring healing, redemption and flourishing to communities around the world?
Imagine what could be done.

Business leaders have great skills. They are the best at getting the
most out of a little. They can organize and deploy resources with remarkable efficiency. They tend to be optimistic and willing to take
calculated risks. They are trained to look for possibilities where others
just see problems. They are trained to look for a third option—the creative win-win solution that can break through deadlocks. And they
often have the capacity to gather substantial resources to direct toward
needed solutions. Big challenges motivate them and they tend to perse-

---

[36]Based on World Bank Development Indicators 2008. Note that in August 2008, the World
Bank revised its international standard for extreme poverty up from $1 a day to $1.25 a day.
See in particular Shaohua Chen and Martin Ravallion, "The Developing World Is Poorer
Than We Thought, But No Less Successful in the Fight Against Poverty," World Bank, Au-
gust 2008; Martin Ravallion, Shaohua Chen and Prem Sangraula, "Dollar a Day Revisited,"
World Bank, May 2008.
[37]"The State of the World's Children 2008," UNICEF, December 2007 <www.unicef.org/
sowc08/docs/sowc08.pdf>.

vere in the face of tremendous odds when convinced that they are on the right path.

The business of business is to serve the world. The world needs business, and business matters to God. "Ask the Lord of the harvest, therefore, to send out workers into his harvest field" (Luke 10:2).[38]

---

[38]If you have questions, would like to contact the author or want access to further related information please see <www.spu.edu/depts/sbe/WhyBusinessMatterstoGod/>.

# Author Index

# Subject Index

# Scripture Index